Canada
And
The Canadians
Vol. 2

by

Sir Richard Henry Bonnycastle

Double 9
BOOKS

Canada And The Canadians
Vol. 2
by Sir Richard Henry Bonnycastle

ISBN: 978-93-59392-55-4

Published by

DOUBLE 9 BOOKS

2/13-B, Ansari Road
Daryaganj, New Delhi – 110002
info@double9books.com
www.double9books.com
Tel. 011-40042856

ABOUT THE AUTHOR

Sir Richard Henry Bonnycastle is an accomplished author known for his insightful and engaging literary works. With a passion for history, culture, and exploration, Bonnycastle has dedicated his writing career to shedding light on various aspects of Canadian society and identity. His works, including "Canada and the Canadians, Vol-2," showcase Bonnycastle's meticulous research and his ability to weave together facts, personal anecdotes, and vivid descriptions. Through his writing, he paints a comprehensive picture of Canada's diverse landscapes, from its majestic natural wonders to its bustling urban centers. Bonnycastle's writing style is characterized by a careful balance of information and storytelling, making his works accessible to a wide range of readers. He showcases a deep appreciation for Canada's rich heritage, exploring the influences of Indigenous cultures, European colonization, and immigration on the nation's development. As an author, Richard Henry Bonnycastle's contributions have provided invaluable insights into Canada's history, culture, and societal fabric.

CONTENTS

CHAPTER X.

Return to Toronto, after a flight to Lake Superior—Loons natural Diving Bells—Birds caught with hooks at the bottom of Niagara River—Ice-jam—Affecting story—Trust well placed—Fast Steamer—Trip to Hamilton—Kékéquawkonnaby, alias Peter Jones—John Bull and the Ojibbeways—Port Credit, Oakville, Bronte, Wellington Square—Burlington Bay and Canal—Hamilton—Ancaster—Immense expenditure on Public Works—Value of the Union of Canada with Britain, not likely to lead to a Repeal—Mackenzie's fate—Family Compact—Church and Kirk—Free Church and High Church—The Vital Principle—The University—President Polk, Oregon, and Canada.

After a ramble in this very desultory manner, which the reader has, no doubt, now become accustomed to, I returned to Toronto, having first observed that the harvest looked very ill on the Niagara frontier; that the peaches had entirely failed, and that the grass was destroyed by a long drought; that the Indian corn was sickly, and the potatoes very bad. Cherries alone seemed plentiful; the caterpillars had destroyed the apples—nay, to such an extent had these insects ravaged the whole province, that many fruit-trees had few or no leaves upon them. A remarkable frost on the 30th of May had also passed over all Upper Canada, and had so injured the woods and orchards, that, in July, the trees in exposed places, instead of being in full vigour, were crisped, brown, and blasted, and getting a renewal of foliage very slowly.

My return to Toronto was caused by duty, as well as by a desire to visit as many of the districts as I possibly could, in order to observe the progress they had made since 1837, as well as to employ the mind actively, to prevent the reaction which threatened to assail it from the occurrence of a severe dispensation.

I heard a very curious fact in natural history, whilst at Niagara, in company with a medical friend, who took much interest in such matters.

I had often remarked, when in the habit of shooting, the very great length of time that the loon, or northern diver, (colymbus glacialis,) remained under water after being fired at, and fancied he must be a living diving-bell, endued with some peculiar functions which enabled him to obtain a supply of air at great depth; but I was not prepared for the circumstance that the fishermen actually catch them on the hooks of their deepest lines in the Niagara river, when fishing at the bottom for salmon-trout, &c. Such is, however, the fact.

An affecting incident at Queenston, whilst we were waiting for the Transit to take us to Toronto, must be related. I have mentioned that, in the spring of 1845, an ice-jam, as it is called here, occurred, which suddenly raised the level of the Niagara between thirty and forty feet above its ordinary floods, and overset or beat down, by the grinding of mountain masses of ice, all the wharfs and buildings on the adjacent banks.

The barrack of the Royal Canadian Rifles at Queenston was thus assailed in the darkest hours of the night, and the soldiers had barely time to escape, before the strong stone building they inhabited was crushed. The next to it, but on higher ground, more than thirty feet above the natural level of the river, was a neat wooden cottage, inhabited by a very aged man and his helpless imbecile wife, equally aged with himself. This man, formerly a soldier, was a cabinet-maker, and amused his declining years by forming very ingenious articles in his line of business; his house was a model of curious nick-nackeries, and thus he picked up just barely enough in the retrograding village to keep the wolf from the door; whilst the soldiers helped him out, by sparing from their messes occasionally a little nourishing food.

That night, the dreadful darkness, the elemental warnings, the soul-sickening rush of the river, the groaning and grinding of the ice, piling itself, layer after layer, upon the banks of the river, assailed the old man with horrors, to which all his ancient campaigns had afforded no parallel.

He heard the irresistible enemy, slowly, deliberately, and determinedly advancing to bury his house in its cold embrace. He hurried the unmindful sharer of his destiny from her bed, gathered the most precious of his household goods, and knew not how or where to fly. Loudly and oft the angry spirit of the water shrieked: Niagara was mounting the hill.

The soldiers, perceiving his imminent peril, ventured down the bank, and shouted to him to fly to them. He moved not; they entreated him, and, knowing his great age and infirmity, and the utter imbecility of the poor old dame, insisted upon taking them out.

But the man withstood them. He looked abroad, and the glimmering night showed him nothing but ruin around.

"I put my trust in Him who never fails," said the veteran. "He will not suffer me to perish."

The soldiers, awed by the wreck of nature, rushed forward, and took the ancient pair out by strength of arms; and, no sooner had they done so, than the waters, which had been so eager for their prey, reached the lower floor, and a large wooden building near them was toppled over by waves of solid ice. Much of the poor man's ingeniously-wrought furniture was injured; but, although the neighbouring buildings were crushed, cracked, rent, and turned over, the old man's habitation was spared, and he still dwells there, waiting in the sunshine for his appointed time, with the same faith as he displayed in the utter darkness of the storm.

He had built his cottage on land belonging to the Crown; and, in consequence of an act recently passed, he, with many others who had thus taken possession, had been ordered to remove. But his affecting history had gained him friends, and he has now permission to dwell thereon, until he shall be summoned away by another and a higher authority, by that Power in whom he has his being, and in whom he put his trust.

We landed once more at Toronto, at present "The City" of Upper Canada, on the 7th of July, and left it again on the 8th, in the fine and very fast steamer Eclipse for Hamilton, in the Gore district, at three o'clock, p.m. The day was fine; and thus we saw to advantage the whole shore of Ontario, from Toronto to Burlington.

Our first stopping place was Port Credit, a place remarkable for the settlement near it of an Indian tribe, to which the half-bred Peter Jones, or Kékéquawkonnaby, as he is called, belongs.

This man, or, rather, this somewhat remarkable person, and, I think, missionary teacher of the Wesleyan Methodists, attained a share of notoriety in England a few years ago, by marrying a young English woman of respectable connections, and passed with most people in wonder-loving London as a great Indian Chief, and a remarkable instance of the development of the Indian mind. He was, or rather is, for I believe he is living, a clever fellow, and had taken some pains with himself; but, like most of the Canadian lions in London, does not pass in his own country for any thing more than what he is known to be there, and that is, like the village he lives near, of credit enough. It answers certain purposes every now and then to send people to represent particular interests to England; and, in nearly all these cases, John Bull receives them with open arms, and, with his national gullibility, is often apt to overrate them.

The O-jibbeway or Chippewa Indians, so lately in vogue, were a pleasant instance, and we could name other more important personages who have made dukes, and lords, and knights of the shire, esquires of the body, and simple citizens pay pretty dearly for having confided their consciences or their purse-strings to their keeping.

Beware, dear brother John Bull, of those who announce their coming with flourishes of trumpet, and who, when they arrive on your warm hearths, fill every newspaper with your banquetings, addresses, and talks, not to honour you, but to tell the Canadian public what extraordinary mistakes they have made in not having so readily, as you have done, found out their superexcellencies.

These are the men who sometimes, however, find a rotten rung in Fortune's ladder, and thus are suddenly hurled to the earth, but who, if they succeed and return safely, become the picked men of company, forget men's names, and, though you be called John, call you Peter.

The mouth of the little river Credit is called Port Credit, the port being made by the parallel piers run out into deep water on cribs, or frames of timber filled with stones, the usual mode of forming piers in Canada West. It is a small place, with some trade, but the Indians complain sadly that the mills and encroachments of the Whites have destroyed their salmon-fishery, which was their chief resource. Where do the Whites come in contact with the Red without destroying their chief resource? Echo answers, Where?

Sixteen miles farther on we touched at Oakville, or Sixteen Mile Creek, where again the parallel piers were brought into use, to form a harbour. Oakville is a very pretty little village, exhibiting much industry.

Bronte, or Twelve Mile Creek, is the next village, very small indeed, with a pier, and then Port Milford, which is one mile from Wellington Square, a place of greater importance, with parallel piers, a steam-mill, and thriving settlement; near it is the residence of the celebrated Indian chief Brant, who so distinguished himself in the war of 1812. Here also is still living another chief, who bears the commission of major in the British army, and is still acknowledged as captain and leader of the Five Nations; his name is John Norton, or, more properly, Tey-on-in-ho, ka-ra-wen.

That which I wished particularly, however, to see, was now close to us, the Canal into Burlington Bay.

Burlington Bay is a little lake of itself, surrounded by high land in the richest portion of Canada, and completely enclosed by a bar of broad sand and alluvial matter, which runs across its entrance. In driving along this belt, you are much reminded of England: the oaks stand park-like wide asunder, and here, on tall blasted trees, you may frequently see the bald eagle sitting as if asleep, but really watching when he can rob the fish-hawk of the fruits of his piscatory toils.

The bald eagle is a cunning, bold, bad bird, and does not inspire one with the respect which his European congeners, the golden or the brown eagle, do. He is the vulture of North America rather than the king of birds. Why did Franklin, [1] or whoever else did the deed, make him the national emblem of power? He is decidedly a mauvais sujet.

The Canal of Burlington Bay is an arduous and very expensive undertaking. The opening from Lake Ontario was formerly liable to great changes and fluctuations, and the provincial work, originally undertaken to fix the entrance more permanently, was soon found inadequate to the rapid commercial undertakings of the country. Accordingly, a very large sum was granted by the Parliament for rendering it stable and increasing the width, which is now 180 feet, between substantial parallel piers.

There is a lighthouse at each end on the left side going in, but the work still requires a good deal of dredging, and the steamboat, although passing slowly and steadily, made a very great surge. In fact, it requires good steerage-way and a careful hand at the helm in rough weather.

The contractors made a railroad for five miles to the mountain, to fetch the stone for filling-in the piers.

The voyage across Burlington Bay is very pleasant and picturesque, the land being more broken, elevated, and diversified than in the lower portions of Canada West; and the Burlington Heights, so important a position in the war of 1812, show to great advantage. Here is one of the few attempts at castle-building in Canada called Dundurn Castle, the residence of Sir Allan Macnab. It is beautifully situated, and, although not perhaps very suitable to a new country, it is a great ornament to the vicinity of Hamilton, embowered as it is in the natural forest. Near it, however, is a vast swamp, in which is Coot's Paradise, so named, it is said, from a gentleman, who was fond of duck-shooting, or perhaps from the coot or water-hen being there in bliss.

Hamilton is a thriving town, exhibiting the rapid progress which a good location, as the Americans call it, ensures. The other day it was in the forest, to-day it is advancing to a city. It has, however, one disadvantage, and that is the very great distance from its port, which puts both the traveller and the merchant to inconvenience, causing expense and delay. How they manage, of a dark night, on the wharf to thread the narrow passage lined with fuel-wood for the steamboat I cannot tell; but, in the open daylight of summer, I saw a vehicle overturned and sent into the mud below. There is barely room for the stage or omnibus; and thus you must wait your turn amidst all the jostling, swearing, and contention, of cads, runners, agents, drivers, and porters; a very pleasant situation for a female or an invalid, and expecting every moment to have the pole of some lumber-waggon driven through your body.

Private interest here, as well as in so many other new places and projects in Canada, has evidently been at work, and a city a mile or two from its harbour, without sufficient reason, has been the result. But that will change, and the city will come to the port, for it is extending rapidly. The distance now is one mile and a quarter.

After great delay and a sharp look-out for carpet-bags and leather trunks, we arrived at Young's Hotel, a very substantial stone building, on a large scale, where civility and comfort made up for delay. It was English.

As it was night before we got settled, although a very fine night, and knowing that I should start before "Charles's Wain was over the new chimney," I sallied forth, with a very obliging guide, who acted as representative of the commissariat department, to examine the town.

The streets are at present straggling, but, as in most Canadian new towns, laid out wide and at right angles. The main street is so wide that it would be quite impracticable to do as they do in Holland, namely, sit at the door and converse, not sotto voce, with your opposite neighbour. It is in fact more like a Mall than a street, and should be planted with a double row of trees, for it requires a telescope to discover the numbers and signs from one row of houses and shops to the other.

Here the American custom of selling after dark by lamplight was everywhere visible, and everywhere new stone houses were building. I went into Peest's Hotel, now Weeks's, the American Tavern, and there saw indubitable signs that the men of yore had a pretty sprinkling of Yankees among them.

Hamilton has 4500 inhabitants, and is a surprising place, which will reach 10,000 people before two or three years more pass. It has already broad plank-walks, but they are not kept in very good repair; in fact, it cannot escape the notice of a traveller from the Old World that there is too magnificent a spirit at work in the commencement of this place, and that utility is sacrificed to enlargement.

Hamilton is beautifully situated on a sloping plane, at the foot of a wooded range of hills, called mountains, whence fine stone of very white colour in immense blocks is easily procured and brought; and it is very surprising that more of this stone has not been used in Toronto, instead of wood. Brick-clay is also plentiful, and excellent white and red bricks are made; but, such is the rage for building, that the largest portion of this embryo city is of combustible pine-wood.

I left Hamilton in a light waggon on the 9th of July, at half-past five o'clock, a.m., having been detained for horses, and rolled along very much at my ease, compared to what the travelling on this route was seven years ago—I was going to say, on this road, but it would have been a misnomer, for there was nothing but a miry, muddy, track then: now, there is a fine, but too narrow, macadamized highway, turnpiked—that is to say, having real turnpike gates.

The view from "the mountain" is exceedingly fine, almost as fine as that from Queenston heights, embracing a richly-cultivated fruit and grain country, a splendid succession of wooded heights, and a long, rolling, ridgy vista of forest, field, and fertility, ending in Lake Ontario, blue and beautiful.

We arrived, at a quarter past seven, at Ancaster, a very pretty little village, with two churches, and composed principally of wooden houses.

The Half-way House is then gained, being about half a mile from the end of the macadamized road, and thirteen and a half from Hamilton. Good bridges, culverts, and cutting, are seen on this section of the line to London. We got to Ancaster at half-past eight, or in about two hours and three quarters, and thence over the line of new road which was, what is called in America, graded, that is, ploughed, ditched, and levelled, preparatory to putting on the broken stone, and which graded road, in spring and autumn, must be very like the Slough of Despond.

At eleven, we reached Maloney's Tavern—most of the taverns on the Canadian new roads are kept by Irish folks— four miles from Brentford.

The Board of Works have been busily employed here, for a great portion of the road is across a swamp, which has been long known as the swamp. This is a pine-country, soil, hard clay or mud, and no stone; and the route is a very expensive one to form, requiring great bridging and straightening.

I observe that the estimate for 1845, for Public Works on this road, in the Gore District, for finishing it, is as high as £10,000 currency, and it is to be all planked, and that, to continue it to London, £36,182 15s. 8d. had been expended up to July, 1844.

The immense expenditure, since 1839, upon internal improvements in Canada, in canals, harbours, lighthouses, roads, &c., is almost incredible, as the subjoined list will show:—

REPORT OF THE BOARD OF WORKS,

SHOWING THE MONEYS EXPENDED UPON EACH OF THE PUBLIC WORKS, FROM THE COMMENCEMENT OF THE WORK, UP TO THE 1ST JULY, 1844.

Welland Canal	£238,995	14	10
ST. LAWRENCE CANALS, VIZ.:			
Prescott to Dickenson's landing	13,490	19	4
Cornwall (to the time of opening the Canal in June, 1843)	57,110	4	2
Cornwall (to repair breaks in the banks since the above period)	9,925	16	4
Beauharnois	162,281	19	5
Lachine	45,410	11	2
Expenditure on dredge, outfit, &c., applicable to the foregoing in common	4,462	16	3
Lake St. Peter	32,893	19	3
Burlington Bay Canal	18,539	11	2
Hamilton and Dover Road	30,044	16	5
NEWCASTLE DISTRICT, VIZ.:			
Scugog Lock and Dam	6,645	8	1
Whitlas Lock and Dam	6,101	7	11
Crook's Lock and Dam	7,849	9	6
Heely's Falls	8,191	5	1
Middle Falls	219	2	8
Ranney's Falls	228	6	8
Chisholm's Rapids	7,599	14	0
Harris's Rapids	1,591	9	6
Removing sundry impediments in the River	185	17	0

Port Hope and Rice Lake Road	1,439	16	4
Bobcaygean, Buckhorn, and Crook's Rapids	12	0	0
Applicable to the foregoing works generally	6,674	1	2

HARBOURS, AND LIGHTHOUSES, AND ROADS LEADING THERETO.

Windsor Harbour	15,355	18	3
Cobourg Harbour	10,381	6	3
Port Dover	3,121	10	4
Long Point Lighthouse and Light-ship	2,163	8	5
Burwell Harbour and Road	136	10	0
Scugog Road	1,202	6	3
Port Stanley	16,242	10	10
Rondeau Harbour, Road and Lighthouse	60	4	2
Port Stanley Road	24,385	13	5
Expenditure on outfit, &c. applicable to the foregoing in common	2,328	13	7
River Ottawa	35,603	16	3
Bay of Chaleurs Road	15,726	16	11
Gosford Road	10,801	10	10
Main North Toronto Road	686	19	4
Bridges between Montreal and Quebec	20,860	19	11
Cascades Road	13,287	19	6
London and Sarnia Road	19,837	5	11
London and Brantford Road	36,182	18	5
London and Chatham, Sandwich and Amherstburgh Road	12,789	0	1
River Richelieu	92	4	0

Certified to be a true abstract of the accounts of the Board of Works.

Thomas A. Begly,

Sec. Board of Works.

Hamilton H. Killarly,

President Board of Works.

The estimate for 1845 was 125,200, as may be seen by the following report of the Inspector General of Canada, as laid before Parliament:—

PUBLIC WORKS.
CANADA WEST.

For present repairs to the Chatham Bridge	£100
For improving the Grand River Swamp Road— total 10,000—required this year	9,000
For improving Rouge Hill and Bridge, also another bridge and hill east of the former— total £6,500— required this year	5,000
For Belleville Bridge	1,500
For the completion of the Dover Road over the mountain, to the limits of the town of Hamilton, and erection of toll-gates	5,500
For the improvement of the road from L'Original to Bytown, by Hattfield, Gifford, Buckworth, and Green's Creeks, as surveyed and estimated, together with the building of a bridge across the narrow channel, at the mouth of the Rideau, on the line of the road from Gattineau Ferry to Bytown—total cost, £5,930—required this year	3,000
Owen's Sound Road, comprehending the line from Dundas by Guelph, to Owen's Sound direct (this sum being for the chopping, clearing, drawing, and forming of the portion not yet opened, and towards the lowering of hills, or otherwise improving such	

bad parts of the line between Nicolet and Dundas
as most require it)   4,000

  For opening the road throughout from Lake Ontario,
at Windsor Harbour, to Georgius Bay, on
Lake Huron, this sum being for the opening of the
road from the head of Scugog Road to the Narrow's
bridge   2,000

  For improving Queenston and Grimsby Road,
for laying on the metal already delivered, and completing
such parts left unfinished as are most advanced,
and establishing gates   8,000

  (To finish the remainder of this communication
within the Niagara district will cost £16,000, and
that within the Gore district £10,000.)

  For improving the Trent navigation, towards the
completion of the works now in progress £12,000—
for this year   6,000

  To cover expense of surveys, examination, preparation
of estimates of the cost of improving the Main
Province Road across the ravines of the Twelve and
Sixteen Mile Creeks between Toronto and Hamilton;
opening a road from the main road to Port Credit;
opening and completing a road from the Ottawa at
Bytown, to the St. Lawrence in the most direct line;
of opening a road between Kingstown and the Lake
des Allumettes on the Ottawa, with a branch towards
the head of the Bay of Quinte; of opening a
road from the Rideau, thence by Perth, Bellamy's
Mills, Wabe Lake, to fall in with the road proposed
from Bytown to Sydenham; of completing
the Desjardin's Canal; of constructing the Murray
Canal; of overcoming the impediments to the navigation
of the river Trent, between Heely's Falls and
the Bay of Quinte, and also for a survey of the
road from Barrie to Lake Huron, through the
townships of Sunindale and Nottawasaga   2,000

For improving the Amherstburgh and Sandwich road	1,000
For the Cornwall and L'Original road	900
	— — — —
	£47,000

WORKS OF A GENERAL CHARACTER,
AS CONNECTED WITH
THE COMMERCE OR REVENUE OF THE COUNTRY.

To forming a dam across the branch of the Mississisqui, and forming a portage road at the Chats	1,250
For works upon the Ottawa and roads connected therewith, as detailed in the Report of the Board of Works of 3rd February, 1845, laid before the legislature—total £21,600—required this year	8,500
For building a landing-wharf, with stairs and approaches at the Quarantine Station, Grosse Isle	2,750
For the extension of piers, and opening inner basin at Port Stanley harbour—total £6,000—required this year	1,200
For dredging at Cobourg harbour	500
For expenses of piers and dredging at Windsor harbour	2,000
For repairs and erection of Lighthouses—total £7,900—this year	5,000
For the formation of a deep water-basin, at the entrance of the Lachine Canal, in the harbour of Montreal, to admit vessels from sea	15,000
For the erection of a Custom House at Toronto	2,500
	— — — —
	£39,700
	— — — —
Total currency	£125,200
	— — — —

W. B. Robinson,

Inspector General.

Thus, from the commencement of the operations of the Board of Works in the Canadas, or in about six years, there will have been no less an amount than a million and a half expended in opening the resources of that "noble province," as Lord Metcalfe styled it, in his valedictory address.

This, with the enormous outlay of nearly two millions during the revolt, the cost of the Rideau Canal and fortifications, and the money spent by an army of from 8 to 10,000 men, has thrown capital into Canada which has caused it to assume a position which the most sanguine of its well-wishers could never have anticipated ten years ago.

Its connection with England, therefore, instead of being a "baneful" one, as a misinformed partizan stated, has been truly a blessing to it, and proves also, beyond a doubt, that, now it is about to have an uninterrupted water-communication from the oceans of Europe, Asia, and Africa, to the fresh-water seas of Ontario, Erie, Huron, Michigan, and Superior, its resources will speedily develop themselves; and that its people are too wise to throw away the advantages they possess, of being an integral portion of the greatest empire the world ever had, for the very uncertain prospects of a union with their unsettled neighbours, although incessant underhand attempts to persuade them to join the Union are going on.

Taxation in Canada is as yet a name, and a hardship seldom heard of and never felt. Perfect freedom of thought in all the various relations of life exists; there is no ecclesiastical domination; no tithes. The people know all this, and are not misled by the furious rhodomontades of party-spirit about rectories, inquisitorial powers, family compacts, and a universal desire for democratic fraternization; got up by persons who, with considerable talents, great perseverance and ingenuity, ring the changes upon all these subjects, in hopes that any alteration of the form of government will place them nearer the loaves and fishes, although I verily believe that many of the most untiring of them would valiantly fight in case of a war against the United States.

A more remarkable example, I believe, has never been recorded in history than the fate of William Lyon Mackenzie, a man possessing an acuteness of mind, powers of reasoning, and great persuasiveness, with indefatigable research and industry, such as rarely fall to obscure and ill-educated men.

Involving Canada in a civil war, which he basely fled before, as soon as he had lighted its horrid torch; as soon, in fact, as he had murdered an old officer, whose services had extended over the world, and who was just on the verge of what he hoped would be a peaceful termination of his toils in his country's cause; as soon as he had burned the houses of a widow who had never offended him, and of a worthy citizen, whose only crime in his eyes was his loyalty; and as soon as he had robbed the mail, and a poor maidservant travelling in it, of her wages. This man fled to the United States, was received with open arms, got a ragged army to invade Canada, then in profound peace with the citizens, who protected him.

His failure at Navy Island is known too well to need repeating. He wandered from place to place, sometimes self-created President or Dictator of the Republic of Canada, sometimes a stump orator, sometimes in prison, sometimes a printer, sometimes an editor, abusing England, abusing Canada, abusing the United States; then a Custom-house officer in the service of that Republic; then again a robber, a plunderer of private letters, left by accident in his office, which he, without scruple, read, and without scruple, for political purposes, published.

Reader, mark his end. It teaches so strong a lesson to tread in the right path that it shall be given in his own words, in a letter which he wrote, on the 11th of November last year, to the "New York Express" newspaper.

He would be pitied, indeed, were it not that the widow and the orphan, the houseless and the maimed, cry aloud against the remorseless one. How many there are now living in Canada, whose lives have been rendered miserable, from their losses, or from injured health, during the watchings and wardings of 1837, 1838, 1839, during the long winter nights of such a climate, during the rains and damps of the spring and of the fall time of the year, and during the heats of an almost tropical summer. Heat, wet, and cold, in all their most terrible forms, were they exposed to. The young became prematurely old. The old died. Peace to their souls! Requiescant in pace!

In the "New York Express" of the 11th November, we find a letter signed by Mr. Mackenzie, in which he endeavours to justify himself. What has particularly engaged our attention are the following paragraphs:—

"If an angel from heaven had told me, eight years ago, that the time would come in which I would find myself an exile, in a foreign land—poor, and with few friends—calumniated, falsely accused, and the feelings of honest, faithful Republicans artfully excited against me—and that among the foremost of my traducers and slanderers would be found Edwin Croswell and the 'Argus,' Thomas Ritchie and his journal, Green and the 'Boston

Post,' with the Pennsylvanian and other newspapers called Democratic; and that these presses and their editors would eagerly retail any and every untruth that could operate to my prejudice, but be dumb to any explanation I might offer, I could not have believed it. But if a pamphlet (like mine) had been then written, exhibiting, with unerring accuracy, the true characters of the combination of unprincipled political managers, among whom you have long acted a conspicuous part; if a Jesse Hoyt had come forward as state's evidence to swear to the truth of the pamphlet, while the parties implicated remained silent; and if you and your afflicted presses had, as you do now with the letters in my pamphlets, defended the real criminals, declared solemnly that you could see nothing wrong in what they had done, and directed the whole force of your widely circulated journal against the innocent person who had warned his countrymen against a most dangerous cabal of political hypocrites of the basest class—in other words, had I known you and your partnership as well in October, 1837, as I do, by dear-bought experience, in November, 1845, I would have hesitated very long indeed, before assuming any share whatever in that responsibility which might have given you the Canadas, as an additional theatre for the exhibition of those peculiar talents, by which this State and Union, and thousands in other lands, have so severely suffered. While reproving gambling and speculation in others, you and your brother wire-pullers have made the property, the manufactures, the commerce of America, your tributaries— even the bench of justice, with its awful solemnities and responsibilities, has been so prostituted by your friends that, when at sea and about to launch three of his fellow-creatures into eternity, a captain in the American navy hesitated not to avow that he had told one of them 'that for those who had money and friends in America there was no punishment for the worst of crimes.'—Nor did the court-martial before whom that avowal was freely made censure him.

"Observe how Mr. and Mrs. Butler sneer at poor judges, corrupt judges, pauper judges, partial chancellors, and at the administration of American justice, though by their own party—and how their leader pities Marcy, throws him on the Supreme Court bench as a stopping place, to save him from ruin.—Look at the bankrupt returns of this district alone—one hundred and twenty millions of dollars in debt, very little paid or to be paid, many of the creditors beggared, many of the debtors astonishing the fashionable with their magnificent carriages and costly horses. No felony in you and your friends, who brought about the times of 1837-8. Oh, no! All the felony consists in exposing you. Two hundred years ago it was a felony to read the Bible in English. Truth will prevail yet.

"I confess my fears that, as I have now no press of my own, nor the means to get one, and am persecuted, calumniated, harassed with lawsuits, threatened with personal violence, saying nothing of the steady vindictiveness of your artful colleague, nor of the judges chosen by Mr. Van Buren and his friends, whom the 'Globe Democratic Review' and 'Evening Post' denounced in 1840, and declared to be independent of common justice and honesty, you may succeed in embittering the cup of misery I have drunk almost to the dregs. The Swedish Chancellor, Count Axel Oxenstiern, wrote to one of his children, 'You do not know yet, my son, how little wisdom is exhibited in ruling mankind.' I think that Mr. Butler cannot be a pure politician, and yet the corrupt individual whose dishonesty I have so clearly shown.—Perhaps the United States government may justify him, and the laws punish me for exhibiting him in his true colours. Be it so—I had for many years an overflow of popularity; and if it is now to be my lot to be overwhelmed with obloquy, hatred, and ceaseless slander, I am quite prepared for it, or even for worse treatment. Being old, and not likely at any future time to be a candidate for office, it is of very little consequence to society what may become of me—but I have a lively satisfaction that I was an humble instrument selected, at a fortunate moment, to prove, by their own admission in 1845, every charge I had made against you and your friends through the 'New York Examiner,' before I left the service of the Mechanics' Institute here, in 1845.

"W. L. Mackenzie."

The Upper Canadians should follow the example of the good people of Amherstburgh, and erect a monument in the capital of Upper Canada to the memory of those who died in consequence of the folly, the hardihood, and the presumption of this man.

There may have been some excuse pleaded for the Canadian French. Misled by designing men, these excellent people of course fancied that, contrary to all possible reason and analogy, a population of about half a million was strong enough to combat with British dominion. Their language, laws, and religion, they were told, were in danger.

But what excuse could the Upper Canadians have—men of British birth, or direct descent, who had grievances, to be sure, but which grievances resolved themselves into the narrow compass of the Family Compact and the thirty-seven Rectories? Quiet farmers, reposing in perfect security under the Ægis of Britain, were the mass of Upper Canadians.

The "Family Compact" is still the war-cry of a party in Upper Canada; and one person of respectability has published a letter to Sir Allan Macnab, in which he states that, so long as the Chief Justice and the Bishop of Toronto continue to force Episcopalianism down the throats of the people, so long will Canada be in danger. This gentleman, an influential Scotch merchant of Toronto, in his letter dated Hamilton, C. West, 18th November, 1846, says, that the Family Compact, or Church of England tory faction, whose usurpations were the cause of the last rebellion, will be the cause of a future and more successful one, "if they are not checked;" and, while he fears rebellion, he dreads that, in case of a war, his countrymen, "the Scotch, could not, on their principles, defend the British government, which suffers their degradation in the colony."

This plainly shows to what an extent party spirit is carried in Canada, when it suffers a man of respectability and loyalty coolly to look rebellion in the face as an alternative between his own church and another.

A Church of England man, totally unconnected with colonial interests and with colonial parties, is a better judge of these matters than a Church of Scotland man, or a Free Church man, who believes, with his eyes shut, that Calvinism is to be thrust bodily out of the land by the influence of Dr. Strachan or Chief Justice Robinson.

It is obvious to common sense that any attempt on the part of the clergy or the laity of Upper Canada to crush the free exercise of religious belief, would be met not only with difficulties absolutely insurmountable, but by the withdrawal of all support from the home government; for, as the Queen of England is alike queen of the Presbyterian and of the Churchman, and is forbidden by the constitution to exercise power over the consciences of her subjects throughout her vast dominions; so it would be absurd to suppose for a moment that the limited influence in a small portion of Canada of a chief justice or a bishop, even supposing them mad or foolish enough to urge it, could plunge their country into a war for the purposes of rendering one creed dominant.

The Church of England is, moreover, not by any means the strongest, in a physical sense, in Upper Canada, neither is the Church of Scotland; nor is it likely, as the writer quoted observes, that it would be at length necessary to sweep the former off the face of the country, in order to secure freedom for the latter.

The Kirk itself is wofully divided, in Canada, by the late wide-spread dissent, under the somewhat novel designation of the Free Church. One need but visit any large town or village to observe this; for it would seem usually that the Free Church minister has a larger congregation than the regularly-called minister of the ancient faith of Caledonia. Now, the members of the Free Church have no such holy horror of Dr. Strachan, Chief Justice Robinson, or Sir Allan Macnab, as that exhibited in the above-mentioned letter; nor is it believed that the Church of England would presume to denounce and wage internecional war against their popular institution. But a person who has lived a great part of his life in Canada will take all this cum grano salis.

The Scotch in Upper Canada are not and will not be disloyal. On the contrary, if I held a militia command again, I should be very glad, as an Englishman, that it should consist of a very fair proportion of Highlanders and of Lowlanders.

The British public must not be misled by the hard-sounding language and the vast expenditure of words it may have to receive, in the perusal of either the High Church, or the Presbyterian fulminators in Canada West.

The whole hinges on what the writer calls "the vital question," namely, upon the university of Canada at Toronto being a free or a close borough.

The High Church party contend that this institution was formed for the Church of England only, and endowed with an immense resource in lands accordingly.

The Church of Scotland, "as by law established," for I do not include the Free Church, has strenuously opposed this for a long series of years, and contends that it has equal rights and equal privileges in the institution. [2]

It would consume too much space to enter into argument upon argument anent a question which, ever since the rebellion, has grown from the seeds so profusely scattered in the grounds of dispute on both sides.

The home government, foreseeing clearly that this vexed question is one of paramount importance, has declared itself not neuter, but passive; has given at large its opinion, favourable to general education, conducted upon the most liberal acceptance of the charter; and has left it to the wisdom of the Canadian Parliament to decide.

An eminent lawyer was employed to carry out Lord Metcalfe's conciliatory views, in accordance with the spirit of the instructions from the queen. This gentleman, who had previously been accused by the reform party of belonging to the Family Compact before he accepted high legal office under the colonial government, had been employed also on the part of the Church of England as counsel before the bar of the House, to advocate its claims, and in a singularly clever and lucid speech, of immense length, certainly made the cause a most excellent one. But

> "how chances mock,
>
> And changes fill the cup of alteration!"

He was lauded to the skies, and deemed to have achieved the great end sought by the High Church party.

Mark the reverse:

They forgot wholly that, in his capacity of barrister, he did, as every barrister is bound to do, his very best for his employers, and no doubt conscientiously desiring that the rights of the Church of England should be upheld; but no sooner was he employed as a minister of the Crown to pacify the discontent which the Presbyterians, the Methodists, and the Roman Catholics had expressed very openly, and no sooner did he, by an equal exertion of his intellect, point put the most feasible method of solving the difficulty, than a storm of abuse most lavishly bespattered him, and he was called a seceder from the High Church principles, an abandoner of the High Canadian Tory ranks, or anything else the reader may fancy. Now, those who know this gentleman best are of opinion that he never was a very violent partizan either in politics or in religious matters, and that to his moderation much of the good that has unquestionably resulted from Lord Metcalfe's government may be ascribed.

The chief justice and the bishop, against whom the tirade of the revolutionary press is constantly aimed, may both have once, by their position in the Upper House, had much to do with political matters, but that either of them has ever had in view so absurd a notion as that of governing Canada by their local influence, and of thus overawing the Crown, is too ridiculous to be believed.

The chief justices and the bishops, in all our colonial possessions, are now most wisely debarred from exercising political sway in the legislative council, over which, some years ago, they no doubt possessed very great influence in many of the colonies.

In Canada, where one half and even more of the population is Roman Catholic, it cannot be believed that a Protestant bishop, or a Protestant head of the civil law, can exercise any other powers than those which their offices permit them to do; and by the British constitution it is very clear that any attempts to subvert the established order of things on their parts would inevitably lead to deprivation and impeachment.

If, therefore, they were really guilty of an endeavour to rule by their family connections, is it probable that 600,000 Roman Catholics, and a vastly preponderating mass of Presbyterians, Methodists, Unitarians, and the endless roll of Canadian dissenters from the Church, would permit it?

That the bishop and the chief justice possess a considerable share of personal influence in Upper Canada, there can be no question whatever; but, after the statement of the former, in his annual visitation published in 1841, that out of a population of half a million there were only ninety-five clergymen and missionaries, where there should be six hundred and thirty-six, if the country was fully settled, it is a fanciful picture that the reformers have drawn of their power and resources—power which is really derived only from intermarriages among the few remnants of the earliest loyalist settlers, or from admiration of their private conduct and abilities. In short, "the family compact" is a useful bugbear; it is kept up constantly before the Canadians, to deter them from looking too closely into other compacts, which, to say the truth, are sometimes neither so national, so loyal, nor so easily explained.

Canada is, at this juncture, without question, the most free and the happiest country in the whole world; not that it resembles Utopia, or the happy valley of Rasselas, but because it has no grievances that may not be remedied by its own parliament—because it has no taxation—because its government is busied in developing its splendid internal resources—and because the Mother Country expends annually enormous sums within its boundaries or in protecting its commerce.

Why does England desire that the banner of the Three Crosses shall float on the citadels of Quebec and Kingston? why does she desire to see that flag pre-eminent on the waters of Lake Superior or in the ports of Oregon? Is it because Canada is better governed as an appanage of the Crown of Victoria than it possibly could be by Mr. Polk? Is it from a mere desire for territory that the mistress of the seas throws her broad shield over the northern portion of North America? or is it because the treasury of England has millions of bars of gold and of silver, deposited in its vaults by the subjects of Canada?

No, it is from none of these motives: Canada is a burthen rather than a mine of wealth to England, which has flourished a thousand-fold more since Washington was the first president, than she ever did with the thirteen colonies of the West.

Is it because the St. Lawrence trade affords a nursery for her seamen, or that Newfoundland is the naval school? No; about three or four British vessels now fish on the grand banks, where hundreds once cast anchor. The fisheries are boat-fisheries on the shores instead of at sea, and the timber trade would engage British shipping and British sailors just as largely if Quebec had the beaver emblazoned on the flag of its fortress as if the flag of a thousand years floated over its walls.

The resources of England are inconceivable; if one source dries up, another opens. China is replacing Africa.

The London Economist estimates the increase of capital in England from 1834, or just before the troubles in Canada, which cost her two millions sterling, to 1844, in ten years only, at the rate of forty-five millions sterling annually—four-hundred and fifty millions, in ten years, in personal property only! What was the increase in real estate during those ten years? and what empire, or what combination of empires, can show such wealth?

Thus, while Canada has been a drag-chain upon the chariot-wheel of British accumulation, did the prosperity of the empire suffer, or is it likely to suffer, by war with the United States, or by separation from England?

The interests of the United States and the interests of England would no doubt mutually suffer, but the former power, if it annexed Canada, would most severely feel the result. England would then close the ports of the St. Lawrence, as well as those of the seaboard from Quebec to Galveston; nor would the Nova Scotian and New Brunswick provinces be conquered until after a bloody and most costly struggle; for they, being essentially maritime, would the less readily abandon the connexion with that power which must for ages yet to come be preponderant at sea. The Ocean is the real English colony. By similar natural laws, the United States has other advantages and other matters to control in its vast interior.

I forget what writer it is who says—perhaps it was Burke—that any nation which can bring 50,000 men in arms into the field, whatever may be its local disadvantages of position, can never be conquered, if its sons are warlike and courageous.

Canada can bring double that number with ease; and whilst its interests are as inseparable from those of England as they now are, it is not to be supposed that a Texian annexation will dissolve the bond.

We have been greatly amused in Canada during the winter of 1845, after Mr. Polk's "all Oregon or none of it," to find in the neighbouring republic a force of brave militia-men or volunteers turn out for a field day with Canada and Oregon painted on their cartouche-boxes.—Mr. Polk did not go quite so far, it is true; but a great mass of the people in the United States prophesy that, if war lasts, all the North American Continent, from the Polar seas to the Isthmus of Darien, will have the tricoloured stripes and the galaxy of stars for its national flag.

This is all-natural enough; no one blames the people of the republic for desiring extended fame and empire; but is it to be extended by the Cæsaric

chiefly however by barter, that true universal medium in a new country, as may be gleaned from any Canadian newspaper about Christmas time, when the subscribers are usually reminded that wood for warming the printer will be very acceptable.

Plank side-walks, a new feature in Canadian towns, are rapidly extending in Brantford, which is just starting into importance; as the government, though it is so far inland, intend to make a port of it, by thoroughly opening the navigation of the Grand River from its mouth in Lake Erie. The works are near completion, and a steamboat, the Brantford, plies regularly in summer. Thus an immense country, probably the finest wheat-land in the world, will be opened to commerce, and the great plaster of Paris quarries of the river find a market, for increasing the fertility of the poorer lands of the lower part of the province.

Brantford is named after Brant, the celebrated Indian warrior chief, and here the Mohawk tribe of the Five Nations have their principal seat. This excellent race, for their adhesion to British principles in the war of the Revolution, lost their territory in the United States, consisting of an immense tract in the fair and fertile valley of the Mohawk river, in the State of New York, through which the Erie Canal and railroad now run, and possessed by a flourishing race of farmers.

I remember being told a curious story of the Dutch, who have their homesteads on the Mohawk Flats, the richest pasture land in New York. These simple colonists, preserving their ancient habits, pipes, breeches, and phlegm, looked with astonishment at the progress of their Yankee neighbours, and predicted that so much haste and action would soon expend itself. At last came surveyors and engineers, those odious disturbers of antiquity and quiet rural enjoyments: they pointed their spirit-levels, they stretched their chains across the fair fields of the quiet slumbering valley of these smoking Dutchmen. The very cows looked bewildered, and Mynheer, taking his meerschaum from his lips, sighed deeply.

They told him that a railroad was projected across his acres; he would not have minded a canal. He had survived the wars of the Indians; he had forgotten Sir William Johnson and his neighbouring castle; he had gone through the rebellion of Washington without being despoiled; and had finally, as he thought, settled down in the lovely valley of the meandering Mohawk, in a flat very like what his ancestors represented to him as the pictured reality of Sluys or Scheldtland. He had smoked and dozed through all this excitement, and was just beginning to understand English. The American character was above his comprehension. He remembered George the Third with respect, because his great grandfather was a Dutchman, who had ascended the British throne, and had proclaimed Protestantism and Orange boven as the law of the colonies. He still thought George the Third his ruler; and never knew that George Washington had, Cromwell-like, ousted the monarch from his fair patrimony, on pretence that tea was not taxable trans-atlantically.

The railroad came: Acts of Congress or of Assembly passed; and fire and iron rushed through the happy valley. The patriarchs lifted up their hands and their pipes in utter dismay.

"Ten thousand duyvels!" exclaimed one old Van Winkle; "vat is dis?— it is too ped! King Jorje is forget himsel. I should not vonder we shall hab a rebublic next."

"I dink ve shall," was the universal response from amidst a dense cloud of tobacco vapour.

The Mohawks, or Kan-ye-a-ke-ha-ka, as they style themselves, are now only a dispersed remnant of a once powerful tribe of the Five Nations. They received several grants of land in Canada for their loyalty, and among others, 160,000 acres of the best part of the province in which we are now travelling, but it is probable that their numbers altogether do not now exceed 3000. Two thousand two hundred dwell near the Grand River, and a large body near Kingston. The Kingston branch are chiefly Church of England men, and an affecting memorial of their adhesion to Britain exists in the altar-cloth and communion-plate which they brought from the valley of the Mohawk, where it had been given to them in the days of Queen Anne.

A church has recently been erected by them on the banks of the Bay of Quinte, in the township of Tyendinaga, or the Indian woods. It is of stone, with a handsome tin-covered spire, and replaces the original wooden edifice they had erected on their first landing, the first altar of their pilgrimage, which was in complete decay.

They held a council, and the chief made this remarkable speech, after having heard all the ways and means discussed:—"If we attempt to build this church by ourselves, it will never be done: let us therefore ask our father, the Governor, to build it for us, and it will be done at once."

It was not want of funds, but want of experience, he meant; for the funds were to be derived from the sale of Indian lands. The Governor, the late Sir Charles Bagot, was petitioned accordingly, and the church now stands a most conspicuous ornament of the most beautiful Bay of Quinte.

They raised one thousand pounds for this purpose; and, proper architects being employed, a contract was entered into for £1037, and was duly accepted. How well it would be if this amount could be refunded to this loyal and moral people from England! What a mite it would take from the pockets of churchmen!

The first stone was laid by S. P. Jarvis, Esq., Chief Superintendent of Indians in Canada; and the Archdeacon of Kingston, the truly venerable G. O. Stuart, conducted the usual service, which was preceded by a procession of the Indians, who, singing a hymn, led the way from the wharf where the clergy and visitors had landed from the steamers, past the old church, through the grounds appropriated for their clergyman's house, and then, ascending the hill westward, they crossed the Indian Graves, and reached the site of their new temple. Te Deum and the Hundredth Psalm were then sung, and the Archdeacon, offering up a suitable prayer, the stone was lowered into its place. The following inscription was placed in this stone:—

To

The Glory of God and Saviour

The remnant of the Tribe Kanyeakehaka,

In token of their preservation by the Divine Mercy,

through Christ Jesus,

In the Sixth Year of our Mother Queen Victoria,

Sir Charles Theophilus Metcalfe, G.C.B.

Being Governor-General of British North America,

The Right Reverend J. Strachan, D.D. and LL.D.,

being Bishop of Toronto,

and the Reverend Saltern Givins,
being in the 13th year

of his Incumbency,

The old wooden fabric having answered its end,

This Corner Stone

of

Christ's Church,

Tyendinaga,

was laid in the presence of
The Venerable George Okill Stuart, LL.D.,
Archdeacon of Kingston,
By Samuel Peters Jarvis, Chief Superintendent of
Indian Affairs in Canada,
Assisted by various members of the Church,
On Tuesday, May 30th, A.D. 1843.
James Howard of Toronto,
Architect; George Brown of
Kingston, Architect,
having undertaken the Supervision of the work,
and John D. Pringle being the Contractor.

A hymn was sung by the Indians and Indian children of the school; the Rev. William Macauley, of Picton, delivered an address, which was followed by a prayer from the Rev. Mr. Deacon, and Collects, after which the Archdeacon pronounced the blessing.

I have recited this because I feel that it will interest a very large body of my countrymen in England, and trust that those who can afford to consider it will not forget the Mohawks of Tyendinaga, in whom I take the more interest from having had them under my command during the troubles of 1838, and of whose loyalty and excellent conduct then I have already informed the reader.

I saw this edifice lately; it is Gothic, with four lancet windows on each side, and buttressed regularly. Its space is 60 feet by 40, with a front tower projecting; and the spire, very pointed and covered with glittering tin, rises out of the dark surrounding woods from a lofty eminence of 107 feet. It is certainly the most interesting public building in Canada West.

I wish some excellent lady would embroider a royal standard or silk union-jack, that the Indians might display it on their tower on high days and holidays. Depend upon it they would cherish it as they have done the ancient memorials of their faith, which date from Queen Anne.

The Indian village near Brantford also boasts of its place of worship; but, although it has its ritual from the Church of England, the clergyman comes from the United States and is paid by the society, called the New England Society. He has lived many years among his flock, and is said to be an excellent man. The Indians are to a man as loyal as those of Tyendinaga.

The Society has a school which it supports also, where from forty to fifty Indian children are taught and have various trades to work at.

They are very moral and temperate, and here may be seen the strange spectacle, elsewhere in the neighbourhood of the white man so rare—of unmixed blood. But the Whites amongst them nevertheless are not of the best sample of the race, as a great number of restless American borderers have fixed their tents near the Grand River, and they have managed to get a good deal of their property and lands, although in Canada it is illegal to purchase land from the Indian races. A superintendent, an old officer in the British army, is stationed with the Five Nations purposely to protect them; yet it is impossible for any one to be aware or to guard against the ruffianly practices of those who think that the Red Man has no longer a right to cumber the earth.

The Five Nations are settling; and it is observed that, whenever they cease to be nomadic, and steadily pursue agriculture and the useful arts, the decrease, so apparent in their numbers before, begins to lessen.

The public works, the great high road to London, and the opening of the navigation of the Grand River, have greatly enhanced the value of their property, whilst at the same time it has brought dangers with those conscienceless adventurers from the bordering States, and from the reckless turbulent Irish canal men, who keep the country in constant excitement, and who, owing no allegiance to Britain or to the American Union, cross over from the States to Canada, or vice versa, as work or whim dictates, carrying uneasiness and dismay wherever they go.

Latterly, however, these worse than savages have been kept in some control by the establishment of a mounted or foot police, and by stationing parties of the Royal Canadian Regiment on their flanks. The military alone can keep them in awe, though they cannot always prevent midnight burnings and atrocities. The French Canadians and the Indians cordially detest these canallers.

I was told a story in passing through Brantford, which shows how the spirit of the lower class of American settlers in this portion of Canada is kept up, since they first openly showed it during the rebellion.

A regiment of infantry, I think the 81st, was marching to relieve another at London, and, on arriving here, weary of the deep sandy or miry roads, the men naturally sought the pumps and wells of the village. A fellow who keeps a large tavern, called Bradley's Inn, hated the sight of the British soldier to that degree, that he locked up his pump of good drinking water and left another open, which was unfit for any purpose.

Lately, I see by the papers, this good Samaritan, who could not find it in his heart to assuage the thirst of a parched throat, or to give even a drop of water to the weary, had his house burnt down by accident. It is a wonder that he had not tried to place it to the account of the soldiers; but, perhaps, he was ashamed, and perhaps, they being at so great a distance as London is, he thought that such an impossibility would not go down. There was, it appears, no water to quench his devouring flame. Fiat justitia!

This part of Canada, and about London, has been a chosen region for American settlers, and also for loafers from the borders of the Republic; and accordingly you observe that which is not obvious in any part of the United States, twenty miles from the St. Lawrence, or the lakes, great pretension to independence and rough rudeness of manner, contrasted by the real independence and quiet bearing of the sons of Britain.

The refugees, or whatever the American border-settlers or adventurers in Canada may be called, are invariably insolent, vulgar, and unbearable in their manners; whilst, away from the frontier, in the United States, the traveller observes no ostentatious display of Republicanism, no vulgar insolence to strangers, unless it be in the bar-room of some wayside tavern, where one is sometimes obliged, as elsewhere, to rest awhile, and where the frequenters may be expected to be not either polite or polished.

The Americans may be said to live at the bar; and yet, in all great cities, the bar of the hotels seldom exhibits anything to offend a traveller, who has seen a good deal of the world; nor do I think that purposed insult or annoyance would be tolerated towards any foreigner who keeps his temper.

So it is all over the world. I remember, as a young man, in the army of Occupation in France, when the soul of the nation was ground to despair, at seeing foreign soldiers lording it in la belle France, that, at Valenciennes, St. Omers, Cambray, and all great towns, constant collisions and duels occurred from the impetuous temper of the half-pay French officers, and yet, in many instances, good sense and firmness avoided fatal results.

I know an officer, who was billeted, the night before one of the great reviews of the allied troops, in a small country tavern, where an Englishman had never before been seen, and he found the house full as it could hold of half-pay Napoleonists. The hostess had but one room where the guests could dine, and even that had a bed in it; and this bed was his billet.

He arrived late, and found it occupied by moustached heroes of the guard, Napoleon's cavalry and infantry demi-soldes, who had rested there to see the review next day, where the battle of Denain was fought over again with blank cartridge.

They were at supper and very boisterous, but, with the innate politesse of Frenchmen, rose and apologized for occupying his bedroom. To go to bed was of course not to be thought of, so he asked to be permitted to join the table; and, after eating and drinking, he found some of the youngest very much disposed to insult him. He watched quietly; at last, toasts were proposed, and they desired him to fill to the brim. The toast they said, after a great deal of improvising, was to the health of the greatest man and the greatest soldier, Napoléon le Grand!—De tout mon cœur, Napoléon le Grand!

This took them by surprise; they had no idea that an Englishman could see any merit in Napoleon.

"Fill your glasses, gentlemen," said the officer, "to the brim, as I filled mine."

They did so, and he said "A la santé de Napoléon deux," which was then a favourite way with the French Imperialists of toasting his son.

The effect was electric. The most insolent and violent of the vieux moustaches took up the stool he was sitting upon and threw it through the window; the glasses followed; and then he went round and embraced the proposer.

"Brave Anglais!" was shouted from many heated lungs; and the evening not only concluded in harmony, but they caused the hostess to make her unwelcome visitor as comfortably lodged for the night as the resources of her house would admit.

Thus it is all over the world; firmness and prudence carry the traveller through among strange people and stranger scenes; and, believe me, none but bullies, sharpers, or the dregs of the populace in any Christian country will insult a stranger.

All the stories about spitting, and "I guess I can clear you, mister," as the man said when he spat across some stage-coach traveller out of the opposite window, are very far-fetched. The Americans certainly do spit a great deal too much for their own health and for other people's ideas of comfort, but it arises from habit, and the too free practice of chewing tobacco. I never saw an American of any class, or, as they term it, of any grade, do it offensively, or on purpose to annoy a stranger. They do it unconsciously, just as a Frenchman of the old school blows his nose at dinner, or as an Englishman turns up his coat-tails and occupies a fireplace, to the exclusion of the rest of the company.

An Englishman should not form his notions of America from the works of professed tourists—men and women who go to the United States, a perfectly new country, for the express purpose of making a marketable book: these are not the safest of guides. One class goes to depreciate Republican institutions, the other to praise them. It is the casual and unbiassed traveller who comes nearest to the truth.

Monsieur de Tocqueville was as much prepossesed by his own peculiar views of the nature of human society as Mrs. Trollope. Extremes meet; but truth lies usually in the centre. It is found at the bottom of the well, where it never intrudes itself on general observation.

The Americans have no fixed character as a nation, and how can they? The slave-holding cavaliers of the South have little in common with the mercantile North; the cultivators and hewers of the western forests are wholly dissimilar from the enterprising traders of the eastern coast; republicanism is not always democracy, and democracy is not always locofocoism; a gentleman is not always a loafer, although certainly a loafer is never a gentleman. A cockney, who never went beyond Margate, or a sea-sick trip to Boulogne, that paradise of prodigals, always fancies that all Americans are Yankees, all clock-makers, all spitters, all below his level. He never sees or converses with American gentlemen, and his inferences are drawn from cheap editions of miserable travels, the stage, or in the liners in St. Katherine's Docks, after the company of the cabin has dispersed.

The American educated people are as superior to the American uneducated as is the case all over Christendom; and John Bull begins to find that out; for steam has brought very different travellers to the United States from the bagmen and adventurers, the penny-a-liners, and the miserables whose travels put pence into their pockets, and who saw as little of real society in America as the poor Vicar of Wakefield's family, before they knew Mr. Burchell.

The Americans you meet with in Canada are, with some exceptions, adventurers of the lowest classes, who, with the dogmatism of ignorant intolerance, hate monarchy because they were taught from infancy that it was naught. Such are the people who lock up their pumps; but they are not all alike. There are many, many, very different, who have emigrated to Canada, because they dislike mob influence, because they live unmolested and without taxation, and because they are not liable every moment to agrarian aggression.

In this part of the Canadas, the runaway slaves from the Southern States are very numerous.

There is an excellent covered bridge over the Grand River at Brantford; and, on crossing this in the waggon, we saw a good-hearted Irishman do what Mr. Bradley refused to do, that is, give drink to a wayfarer.

This wayfarer resembled the Red Coat that Mr. Bradley hated so in one particular—he had his armour on. It was a huge mud turtle, which had most inadvertently attempted to cross the road from the river into the low grounds, and a waggon had gone over it; but the armour was proof, and it was only frightened. So the old Irish labourer, after examining the great curiosity at all points, took it up carefully and restored it to the element it so greatly needed—water. Was he not the Good Samaritan?

Whilst here, we were told that at Alnwick, in the Newcastle district, the government has located an Indian settlement on the Rice Lake very carefully. Each Indian has twenty-five acres of land, and a fine creek runs through the place, on the banks of which the Indian houses have been built so judiciously, that the inhabitants have access to it on both sides.

The Mohawk language is pronounced without opening and shutting the lips, labials being unknown. Some call the real name of the tribe Kan-ye-ha-ke-ha-ka, others Can-na-ha-hawk, whence Mohawk by corruption.

After staying a short time at Clement's Inn, which is a very good one, we left Brantford at half-past one, and were much pleased with the neatness of the place, and particularly with the view near the bridge of the river. The Indian village and its church are down the stream to the left, about two miles from the town, and embowered in woods.

We drove along for eight miles to the Chequered Sheds, a small village so called; at twenty minutes to four reached Burford, two miles further on, which is another small place on Burford Plains, with a church; and at a quarter past four reached a very neat establishment, a short distance beyond a small creek, and called the Burford Exchange Inn. The country is well settled, with good houses and farms.

We stopped a short time at Phelan's Inn, four miles and a half on, just beyond which the macadamized road commences again; but the country is not much settled between the Exchange and Phelan's Inn.

CHAPTER XII.

Woodstock—Brock District—Little England— Aristocratic Society in the Bush—How to settle in Canada as a Gentleman should do—Reader, did you ever Log?—Life in the Bush—The true Backwoods.

We arrived at Woodstock at eight p.m., and were delighted with the rich appearance of the settlement and country, resembling some of the best parts of England, and possessing a good road macadamized from granite boulders.

Woodstock is a long village, neatly and chiefly built of wood, fifty three miles from Hamilton. It is the county town of the Brock district; and here numbers of gentlemen of small fortunes have settled themselves from England and Ireland. It is a thriving place, and their cottages and country houses are chiefly built, and their grounds laid out, in the English style, with park palings. Sir John Colborne has the merit of settling this loyal population in the centre of the western part of Canada.

The old road went through a place called absurdly enough Paris, from the quantity of gypsum with which the neighbourhood abounds; and fine specimens of silurian fossils of the trilobite family and of madrepores, millepores, and corallics, are found here. Love's Hotel is the best in the village, and a good one it is.

What with the truly English scenery of the Oak Plains, the good road, and the British style of settlement, Woodstock would appear to be the spot at which a man tired of war's alarms should pitch his tent; and accordingly there are many old officers here; but the land is dear and difficult now to obtain. A recent traveller says it is the most aristocratic settlement in the province, and contains, within ten miles round, scions of the best English and Irish families; and that the society is quite as good as that of an average country neighbourhood at home. The price of land he quotes at £4 sterling an acre for cleared, and from £1 to £1 10s. for wild land. A friend of his gave £480 for sixty cleared and one hundred uncleared acres, with a log house, barn, and fences.

He moreover gives this useful information, that very few gentlemen farmers do more than make their farms keep their families, and never realize profit: thus, he says, a single man going to Woodstock to settle ought to have at least one hundred pounds a year income quite clear, after paying for his land, house, and improvements.

I have seen a good deal of farming and of farmers in Canada. Farming there is by no means a life of pleasure; but, if a young man goes into the Bush with a thorough determination to chop, to log, to plough, to dig, to delve, to make his own candles, kill his own hogs and sheep, attend to his horses and his oxen, and "bring in firing at requiring," and abstains from whiskey, it signifies very little whether he is gentle or simple, an honourable or a homespun, he will get on. Life in the Bush is, however, no joke, not even a practical one. It involves serious results, with an absence of cultivated manners and matters, toil, hardship, and the effects of seasoning, including ague and fever.

Recipe.—First buy your land in as fine a part of the province as possible, then build your log-hut, and a good barn and stable, with pig and sheep-pens. Then commence with a hired hand, whom you must not expect to treat you en seigneur, and who will either go shares with you in the crops, or require £30 currency a year, and his board and lodging.

Begin hewing and hacking till you have cleared two or three acres for wheat, oats, and grass, with a plot for potatoes and Indian corn.

When you have cut down the giant trees, then comes the logging. Reader, did you ever log? It is precious work! Fancy yourself in a smock-frock, the best of all working dresses, having cut the huge trees into lengths of a few feet, rolling these lengths up into a pile, and ranging the branches and brush-wood for convenient combustion; then waiting for a favourable wind, setting fire to all your heaps, and burying yourself in grime and smoke; then rolling up these half-consumed enormous logs, till, after painful toil, you get them to burn to potash.

Wearied and exhausted with labour and heat, you return to your cabin at night, and take a peep in your shaving-glass. You start back, for, instead of the countenance you were charmed to meet at the weekly beard reckoning, you see a collier's face, a collier's hands, and your smock-frock converted into a charcoal-burner's blouse.

Cutting down the forest is hard labour enough until practice makes you perfect; chopping is hard work also; but logging, logging—nobody likes logging.

Then, when you plough afterwards, or dig between the black stumps, what a pleasure! Every minute bump goes the ploughshare against a stone or a root, and your clothes carry off charcoal at a railroad pace.

It takes thirty years for pine-stumps to decay, five or six for the hard woods; and it is of no use to burn the pine-roots, for it only makes them more iron-like; but then the neighbours, if you have any, are usually kind: they help you to log, and to build your log-hut.

Your food too is very spicy and gentlemanlike in the Bush: barrels of flour, barrels of pork, fat as butter and salt as brine, with tea, sugar—maple-sugar, mind, which tastes very like candied horehound—and a little whiskey, country whiskey, a sort of non-descript mixture of bad kirschwasser with tepid water, and not of the purest goût. Behold your carte. If you have a gun, which you must have in the Bush, and a dog, which you may have, just to keep you company and to talk to, you may now and then kill a Canada pheasant, ycleped partridge, or a wild duck, or mayhap a deer; but do not think of bringing a hound or hounds, for you can kill a deer just as well without them, and I never remember to have heard of a young settler with hounds coming to much good. Moreover, the old proverb says, a man may be known by his followers: and it is as absurd for a poor fellow, without money, to have great ban-dogs at his heels, as it would be for a rich nobleman to live in his garret upon bread and water. Moreover, in Canada, most sportsmen are mere idlers, and generally neglectful either of their professions or of their farms. Many a fine young fellow has been ruined in Canada, by fancying it very fine to copy the officers of the army in their sportsmanship, forgetting that these officers could afford both in time and money what they could not.

Keep your house, and your house will keep you. Almost all settlers too have mothers, wives, sisters, brothers, cousins, to assist them, or to provide for; and, if they are industrious, a few years make them happy and independent.

Even £50 a year of clear income in the Bush is a very pretty sum, and £100 per annum places you on the top of the tree—a magnate, a magistrate, a major of militia.

I know many, many worthy families, who live well with their pensions or their half-pay.

What a luxury to have your own land, two hundred acres!—to live without the chandler, the butcher, the baker, the huxter, and the grocer! Tea, a little sugar and coffee, these are your real luxuries.

Soap you make out of the ley of your own potash; fat you get from your pigs or your sheep, which supply you with candles and food; and by and by the good ox and the fatted calf, the turkey, the goose, and the chicken, give your frugal board an air of gourmandism; whilst in this climate all the English garden vegetables and common fruits require only a little care to bring them to perfection. Indian corn and buckwheat make excellent cakes and hominy; and you take your own wheat to be ground at the nearest mill, where the miller requires no money, but only grist. In like manner, the boards for your house are to be had at the sawmill for logs, for potash, for wheat, for oats.

Keep a few choice books for an evening, and provide yourself with stout boots and shoes, a good coat, and etceteras, besides your smock-frock and shooting-jacket of fustian, and its continuations, and let the rest follow; for you will at last take to wear country homespun, when occasions of state do not require it otherwise, such as church and tea-parties of more than ordinary interest.

People talk about life in the Bush as they do about life in London, without knowing very much about either. Backwoods and backwoodsmen are novelties which amuse for the moment. A backwoodsman, who never worked at a farm, although he may be much in the habit of seeing farmers, has not always just conceptions. He must not live in a village newly made, but actually reside in a log-hut, just erecting, to know what life in the Bush is. Gentlemen and lady travellers are the worst judges possible, because, even if they go and visit their friends, the best foot is always put foremost to receive them, and vanity or love induces every sacrifice to make them comfortable.

They see nothing of the labours of the seven months' winter, of the aguish wet autumn, of the uncertain spring, of the tropical summer, of ice, of frost, of musquitoes and black flies, of mud and mire, of swamp and rock, of all the innumerable drawbacks with which the spirit of the settler has to contend, or the very coarse and scanty fare to solace him after his toils of the day.

See a young pair of brothers, sons of an officer of high rank, whose father dying left them but partially provided for, with a mother and several grown-up daughters.

They fly to France to live. This resource might, by a war, be soon broken up. The sons collect what remains of money—they arrive in Canada. They purchase cheap land far in the interior, miles away from any town. They build a log-hut, clear their land, and accumulate gradually the furniture and household goods. Toil, toil, toil. The log-hut is enlarged. The mother and daughters are invited from home to join their "life in the Bush." They are expected. Everything is made comfortable for them. The brothers are chopping in the woods—night approaches. They return—return to find their log-house, furniture, wardrobe, books, linen—every thing consumed.

They are wanderers in the wilderness. Do they despair? Yes, because one brother, the strongest, takes cold—he lingers, he dies.

The survivor, indomitable, yet bowing under his accumulated afflictions, assisted by his neighbours, builds another log-house. His mother and sisters arrive, are dispersed among the nearest neighbours, get the ague. Struggle, struggle, struggle! on, on, on! The pension here is of service. The girls, brought up in luxury, scions of a good race, turn their hands cheerfully to do every thing. Their conduct is admired. Other settlers from the gentry at home arrive with some capital. The locality turns out good. The girls marry well. The surviving son, ten years afterwards, has four hundred acres of his own—thinks of building a house fit for a gentleman farmer to live in, and is surrounded by broad acres of wheat, without a stump to be seen, with a large flock of sheep grazing peacefully on his green meadows, and cattle enough to secure him from want.

This is one case, under my own eye, and the moral of it is, neither of the sons drank whiskey.

Look at another picture. An officer of respectable rank, young and tired of the service, where promotion is not even in prospect, settles in Canada— he has money. He buys at once a fine tract of forest, converts it by his money into a fertile farm, builds an excellent house, furnishes it, marries.

Knowing nothing of farming, fond of his dogs and his gun, delighted in a canoe and duck-shooting, absent day after day in the deer-tracks, occasionally killing a wolf or a bear, absorbed in sport, he leaves his farm to the sole care of an industrious man, who receives half the crops. He is cheated at every turn; the man buys with the profits land for himself, and leaves him abruptly.

The fine house requires repairs, the fences get out of order, the cattle and the pigs roam wherever they like. Money, too much money, has been laid out. The fine young man perhaps becomes a confirmed drunkard. Voilà le fin!

This is another case under my own observation, and I very much regret indeed to say that, of the class of gentlemen settlers, it is by far more frequent and observable than the first. Habits of shooting beget habits of drinking and smoking; and it is not at all uncommon in the backwoods to see a man whom you have known on the sunny side of St. James's, dressed in the height of fashion, and of most elegant manners, walking along with his pointer and his gun in a smock-frock or blouse, a pipe, a clay-pipe stuck in the ribbon of his hat, and with evident tokens of whiskey upon him.

If he works at his farm, which all who are not overburthened with riches must do, and those that are usually remain in England, he works hard; and then reflect, reader, that chopping and logging, that cradling wheat and ploughing land, are not mere amusements, but entail the original ban, the sweat of the brow—he must every now and then drink, drink, drink. I have seen a man who would otherwise have been a high ornament to society, whose acquirements were very great, and who brought out an excellent library, abandon literature and his army manners, and drink whiskey, not by the glass but by the tumbler. And what is it, you will naturally ask, that can induce a reasoning soul to do thus? Why!—lack of society, want of current information, the long and tedious winter, and the labours of spring and of autumn. In fact, it is "the backwoods," the listlessness of the backwoods, which, like the opposite extreme, the fatuity and blasé life of a great metropolis, causes men to rush into insane extremes to avoid reflection. The mind is dulled and blunted.

The following facts, translated from an interesting article in the "Mélanges Religieux," a Roman Catholic periodical, published in Montreal, in the French language, may be relied on, to show how narrowed the ideas of a man constantly residing in the woods are:—

"There arrived in Montreal, on Wednesday last, young man about twenty years of age, who had come down from Hudson's Bay, without having, during his long journey, stopped in any town, village, or civilized settlement; so that he stumbled into Montreal with as little idea of a town or of civilization as if he had fallen from the moon, for he had lived on the northern shores of the bay, and had but seldom visited the fur-trading establishments. He had only last spring seen, at Abbititi, Messieurs Moreau and Durauquet, the Roman Catholic Missionaries. He was born of Roman Catholic parents, his father being Scotch, his mother Irish. But he had never left the woods nor the life in the wilds, and had never seen a priest before last spring. How strange must have been the emotions in the breast of this young man on finding himself thus suddenly cast into the midst of this large town, as one would throw a bale of furs! He expressed his feelings at the time as partaking more of stupor than of admiration.

"When he had recovered from the confusion of his ideas consequent upon the novelty of his situation, he sought the Bishop's residence, according to the instructions of his father; and at length found himself more at ease, for, understanding his singular position, those he there met with assisted him to collect his scattered thoughts. In answer to the questions addressed to him (he speaks English, and can read and write), he replied that he could not consent to live in such a place; that the noise deafened him, while the crowds of people, running in all directions, agitated and astonished him in a manner he could not explain. He experienced a sensation of suffocation on finding himself enclosed, as it were, in streets of lofty houses; he saw and admired nothing, being every moment in dread of losing himself in the labyrinth of streets, more difficult for him to recognize than the scarcely marked pathways of his native forests. He was not curious to see any thing, and felt only the desire to fly at once, and again to breathe freely, away from what he felt to be the restraints of civilization. He was taken to the cathedral, where he saw the pictures, the paintings on the roof, and all the ornaments of the church—they were explained to him, and he prayed before the high altar and that of the Holy Virgin. He believed all the instructions of the Church, and was sufficiently informed to receive baptism. During his visit to the church, the organ was played, and an explanation was given him of its harmony. In the midst of all these to him surprising novelties, he was asked what was the predominant sensation in his mind; he answered fear, and that his other feelings he was unable to explain.

"This simple child of nature, the naïveté of whose language, emotions, and habits so strongly contrasted with the surrounding artificial civilization, afforded a singular study to those present. However humiliating to our self-love, the conduct of this young man abundantly proved that the civilization of which we are so proud, our buildings, our wealth, our industry, all our activity and noise, do not fill with the admiration we expect those who are brought up far from our opulent cities and our artificial manners. Nature, in these immense solitudes, in these primitive manners, has then charms unknown to us, to be preferred to those which, in our existing state, we find so incomparable. We must here close our reflections, for fear of falling into paradoxes difficult to be avoided in questions of this nature.

"This young man has departed, without regret, and has gone to the township of Raudon, where he has relations. There he will again find forests, and will be able to breathe freely, without fearing that the lofty dwellings of the city will intercept his view of the blue sky and the bright sun which he loves."

Even near population, the settler has, in his way to town and market, to bait his cattle at roadside taverns, where the bar is the place of business, where he meets neighbours, and hears the news of the market and of the world; and the facility with which, throughout Upper Canada, these grog-shops obtain licenses from the magistrates is so great that the evil every day increases.

In towns, this is most particularly observed, and also that, under the designation of "beer-licenses" the most infamous houses for drinking and vice are suffered to exist. It is full time that the parliament interfered with these license-granters, who increase intemperance instead of using their magisterial office to put a stop to it. Father Matthew's principles are much wanted in Canada West.

In Eastern Canada, or, as it is better known, Lower Canada, the contrary is the case. The Canadian French, as a people, are temperate, although the canoe and batteaux men, lumberers and voyageurs, from the lonely and hard lives they lead, drink to excess; yet the Canadian is a sober character.

CHAPTER XIII.

Beachville—Ingersoll—Dorchester—Plank road—Westminster Hall—London—The great Fire of London—Longwoods—Delaware—The Pious, glorious, and immortal Memory—Moncey—The German Flats—Tecumseh—Moravian settlement—Thamesville—The Mourning Dove—The War, the War—Might against Right—Cigar-smoking and all sorts of curiosity—Young Thames—The Albion—The loyal Western District—America as it now is.

I was detained at Woodstock for some time by the sickness of one of the horses. The animal had dropped in his stable after our arrival, and refused to feed; consequently, our driver had to look for another; and a miserable one, at a large price, he got. The intense heat had overpowered the horse.

We departed, however, at half-past six in the morning, on the 10th July, and reached Beachville, five miles westward.

Beachville is a small country village, beautifully situated, and the country between is undulating and rich. The driver pointed out Mr. John Vansittart's house, an English looking residence, with extensive grounds.

A creek, called Hard Creek, runs along the road with several mill-sites on it. It loses itself every now and then in deep woods; and altogether this is the prettiest country I have ever seen in Canada. The land also appears good.

At Beachville are saw, grist, and water-mills on an extensive scale, the best in the country, owned and worked by Scotch people.

The creek called Little Thames is seen also, which runs through the Canada Company's lands to the Forks of the Thames at London. This is a settlement forty years old; consequently, every thing is forward in it.

We then came through an equally fine, old-settled country, to Ingersoll, five miles farther. This is a straggling place of about the same age, with mills and creeks, and a large inn, called the Mansion House (Hoffman's).

We drove on to Dorchester, a small settlement and an old mill-site, about eighteen miles from London, where we stopped to recruit our wretched horse, at half-past ten. Here we breakfasted at a roadside inn, not very good nor very comfortable, but were glad to observe that the plank road commenced again.

A plank road in England would be a curiosity indeed: here it is none: fancy rolling along a floor of thick boards through field and forest for a hundred miles. The boards are covered with earth, or gravel, if it can be had, and this deadens the noise and prevents the wear and tear, so that you glide along pretty much the same as a child's go-cart goes over the carpet. But this will only do where wood is plentiful, and thus the time must come, even in Canada, when gravelled roads or iron rails will supersede it.

The country was poorer in this section, being very sandy, until near the tavern called Westminster Hall; what a name! But the beautiful little river was occasionally in sight in a hollow of woods of the richest foliage. At one place we saw a party of Indians with ponies and goods, going down to a ford, where no doubt their canoes awaited them. Their appearance as they descended was very picturesque, armed as they were with rifles and fowling-pieces, very Salvator Rosaish.

Westminster Hall, where we arrived at ten minutes to two o'clock, and staid an hour to bait, is six miles and a half from London. Cockney land everywhere.

On our approaching the new capital of the London District, we saw evident signs of recent exertions. Fine turnpike-gates, excellent roads, arbours for pic-nic parties, and before us, at a distance, a large wide-spread clearance, in which spires and extensive buildings lifted their heads.

London is a perfectly new city; it was nothing but a mere forest settlement before 1838, and is now a very large, well laid out town. We arrived at five p.m., and put up at a very indifferent inn, the best however which the great fire of London had spared. The town is laid out at right angles, each street being very wide and very sandy, and where the fire had burnt the wooden squares of houses we saw brick ones rising up rapidly. There is now a splendid hotel, (O'Neill's and Hackstaff's) where you may really meet with luxury as well as comfort, for I see, mirabile dictu, that fresh lobsters and oysters are advertised for every day in the season. These come from the Atlantic coast of the United States, some thousand miles or so; but what will not steam and railroad do! We saw a stone church erecting; and there is an immense barrack, containing the 81st regiment of infantry and a mounted company, or, as it is called in military parlance, a battery of artillery.

London was so thickly beset with disaffected Americans during the rebellion, that it was deemed necessary to check them by stationing this force in the heart of the district; and since then the military expenditure and the excellent situation of the place has created a town, and will soon create a large city.

The adjacent country is very beautiful, particularly along the meandering banks of the Thames. I saw some excellent stores, or general shops; and, although the houses, excepting in the main street, are at present scattered, and there is nothing but oceans of sand in the middle, it wants only time to become a very important place. General Simcoe, when he first settled Upper Canada, thought of making it the metropolis, but it is not well situated for that purpose, being too accessible from the United States.

I staid here all night and part of next day; and here I found the disadvantages of an education for the bar; for my bedroom was immediately over it, and it was open the greatest part of the night. Drinking, smoking, smoking, drinking, incessant, with concomitant noise and bad language; which, combined with a necessity for keeping the window open on account of the heat, rendered sleep impossible. I have slept from sheer fatigue under a cannon, or rather very near it, when it was firing, but Vauban himself could not have slept with the thermometer at 100° Fahrenheit over a Canadian tap-room.

I was glad to leave London in Canada West for that reason, and departed the next day in a fresh waggon at half-past five p.m., arriving at the Corners, six miles off, where a bran-new settlement and bran-new toll-gate appeared with a fine cross road, that to the right leading to Westminster, that to the left to Lake Erie. I was sorry that the plank road was finished only to this place; but we had fine settlements all the way.

Then begins a new country, and that most dreary and monotonous of Canadian landscape scenery—the Long Woods. This lasts to Delaware, where we stopped at eight o'clock, on a fine evening, having travelled twelve miles from the Corners.

Here the road suddenly turns from the river to the right; and we drove past Buller's New House, which he is building, to his old stand. It was ancient enough, but respectable; and if the rats and mice and other small deer could only have been persuaded that one had had no sleep the night before and that the weather was intensely hot, we should have done well enough; although some soldiers on a look-out party for deserters, and some travellers, were not at all inclined to sleep themselves, or to let others enjoy the blessings of repose.

Delaware is a very pretty village, and the Indians are settled some seven miles from it. It has a very large and very long bridge over the Thames.

We started, most militarily, at four in the morning of Friday the 12th of July, without recollecting King William, or the Pious, Glorious, and Immortal Memory. But we were to be reminded of it.

Here we saw the labours of the Board of Works in the Great Western Road to much advantage, in deep cuttings and embankments, fine culverts and bridges, with lots of the sons of green Erin—"first flower of the earth, and first gem of the sea"—and their cabins along the line of works, preparing the level for planking.

The country is flat, but very fine and well settled. Quails amused themselves along the road, looking at us from the wooden rail fences, and did not leave their perches without persuasion. The rascals looked knowing, too, as if they were aware that waggoners did not carry guns.

I heard the real whip-poor-will or night-jar last night frequently, sighing his melancholy ditty along the banks of the beautiful Thames. The cry of the Canada quail, which is a very small partridge-like bird, is very plaintive. As we passed them, they gave it out heartily—Phu—Phoo-iey. We arrived at Smith's tavern, seventeen miles, at half-past seven, breakfasted, and stayed until ten, at that miserable place.

We then drove on, and passed Moncey in Caradoc, so named from an Indian tribe. It is a pretty village, where they had just finished a church, whereon banners were flying, which showed us, that if we had forgotten King William, some folks here had not; and, out of bravado, a refugee American had stuck a pocket-handkerchief flag of the Stars and Stripes up at his shop-door, which we prophesied, as evening came, would be pulled down, because orange, blue, and red flags flourished near it. This is an Indian village, into which the Americans and other white traders and adventurers have set foot.

I was charmed with the scenery, consisting of fertile fields, rich woods, the ever-winding Thames and undulating mammillated hills, covered with verdure. Happy Indians, if unhappy Whites were not thrusting you out!

We arrived at one o'clock at Fleming's Inn, much better than the last, twelve miles. Here we rested awhile.—Starting again, the country was found but very little settled, with long tiresome woods, but still beautiful, all nearly oak. We halted at the German Flats, not to get out, for there was no abiding-place, but to look at the ground, where the battle in the last American war took place, in which Tecumseh, the great Tecumseh, met his death, and where Kentucky heroes made razor-straps of his skin.

Seven miles after leaving these immense woods, the valley of the Thames opens most magnificently in a gorge below, and spreads into rich flats to the left, embowered with the most beautiful forest scenery, in which, about a mile off, stand the Moravian church, school, and Indian village. A more lovely spot could not have been selected. There is a large Indian settlement of old date here; and, as we drove along, we passed through two deserted orchards; the road had rendered them useless; and, from which and its neighbourhood, the Indians had retired into their settled village below. Here the forest was gradually regaining the mastery: fruit-trees had become wild, and the Thames ran in a deep bold ravine far below, clothed with aged and solemn trees, willows and poplars, intermixed with oak, beech, ash, and altogether English and park-like. It put me in mind of the opening chapter of "Ivanhoe."

The road was a deep sand; and we stopped a little at Smith's Inn, three miles and a half from our night's halt. Here the soil changes to clay, and the country is not much settled, but is beginning to be so. We saw bevies of quail on the roadside, which the driver cut at with his whip, but they were not disposed to fly. We arrived at Freeman's Inn at half-past six p.m., twelve miles, and brought up for the night at Thamesville, where there is a dam and an extensive bridge, and altogether the preparation for the plank road is a very extraordinary work, embracing much deep cutting. Here all is sand again, but the occasional glimpses of the Thames, as you approach this village, are very fine and picturesque. Squirrels, particularly the ground species, or chippemunk, amused us a good deal by their gambols as we drove along. The village of Thamesville is very small.

Oh, Father Thames, did you ever dream of having ville tacked to your venerable name? But, as the Nevilles have it, ne vile velis.

I amused myself here on a scorching evening with looking about me, as well as the heat would permit; and here I first heard and first saw that curious little Canadian bird, the mourning dove. It came hopping along the ground close to the inn, but the evening was not light enough for me to distinguish more than that it was very small, not so big as a quail, and dark-coloured. It seemed to prefer the sandy road; and, as it had probably never been molested, picked up the oats or grain left in feeding the horses. It became so far domesticated as to approach mankind, although the slightest advance towards it sent it away. My host, a very intelligent man, told me that it always came thus on the hot summer nights; and we soon heard at various distances its soft but exceedingly melancholy call. It appears peculiar to this part of Canada, and is the smallest of the dove kind. I know of nothing to compare with its soft, cadenced, and plaintive cry; it almost makes one weep to hear it, and is totally different from the coo of the turtle dove. When it begins, and the whip-poor-will joins the concert, one is apt to fancy there is a lament among the feathered kind for some general loss, in the stillness and solemnity of a summer's night, when the leaves of the vast and obscure forest are unruffled, when the river is just murmuring in the distance, and the moon emerging from and re-entering the drifting night-cloud, in a land of the mere remnant of the Indian tribes gone to their eternal rest.

This in a contemplative mood forcibly reminds us of that sublime passage of holy writ, wherein that thrilling command is embodied, to "Remember now thy Creator in the days of thy youth, when he shall rise up at the voice of the bird."

The cruel treatment of the aborigines of that half of the world discovered by Columbus rises, on such an occasion, to the memory, with all its force. Here we stood on that soil, a small portion of which has been doled out to them in return for an empire; and here we could not avoid reflecting upon the injustice which has been so unsparingly dealt out to the Indian in that neighbouring Republic instituted to secure freedom and impartial government to all men.

Yes, a nation claiming to be the most powerful under the sun, claiming a common origin, quarrelled for self-government; the mild sway of a limited monarchy was tyranny and bigotry; established laws and a state religion were swept away under a feeling that the child was strong enough to defy the parent. A more perfect form of government was necessary to the welfare of the human race: Washington arose, and a Republic was created. Did it continue in unison with the aspirations and views of that great man? did he think it requisite to extirpate the Red Men? did he forbid the Catholic to exercise the rights of conscience? did he intend that the Conscript Fathers should break their ivory wands, and bow to the dust before plebeian rule? did he imagine, in declaring all men equal, that mind was to succumb before mere matter, that intelligence was to be ground under the foot of physical force?

The Englishman, the true Englishman, and by that word I mean a citizen of England, a Canadian, as well as he born in Britain or Ireland, judges differently; he acknowledges all men equal, and that all have an equal right inherent in them to receive equal protection; but he renders to Cæsar the things that are Cæsar's, and as he loves his own self, so loves he the representative of every soul bearing the proud name of a British subject.

He well knows, from the experience of all history, sacred and profane, that it is by maintaining order, in the institution of divers ranks in society and in government, that the true balance of power is found; and he feels that, if once that power is obtained by either extreme of the scale, his liberty, both of mind and of body, is at an end.

of sufficient power and resources be kept in the Pacific to counteract and send supplies? He who knows the western wilds well knows that once concentrate Indian warfare, and it would be impossible to keep together or to supply such an army as that of the Republic, unsupported, as it must necessarily be, by a fleet.

The time is coming, and that rapidly, there can be no doubt, when the white man will possess exclusively the Pacific coast; but this is to be achieved by the commercial and not by the physical power, and that it is yet very distant when any one nation will obtain it is the belief of all reasoning people; for even should the Americans force Mexico from its proper station, should they obtain California and Oregon, will Russia look quite quietly on, will France see her great scheme of Pacific colonization in danger, and will England tamely submit to have her eastern territories and the new trade with China put in jeopardy?

I think not, and also conceive that it is as impossible for the United States to support a lengthened war with any great European power as it is for any great European power to conquer or to subdue any portion of the United States.

Spain too is gradually recovering from the shock, which the loss of her Ophir inflicted on her; more liberal notions are gaining ground in Iberia; and it is by no means impossible, that, backed by France, she may yet resume her power in America. Look at the tenacity with which, amidst all her reverses, she has held on to Cuba.

There is, in fact, no surmising the results of a mad war on the part of America.

But, in all their profound calculations, the Indian, the poor despised Indian, is forgotten. How he is to live, how he is to die, are alike matters of indifference.

Well may the mourning dove haunt the villages of the Five Nations!

Thamesville—how I detest the combination! it must have been named in the very spirit of gin-sling—is a place very likely to become of importance when the great western road is quite completed.

I was listening to the mourning dove, which then gave a balm to my wounded spirit, when I observed on the bench under the verandah, or stoup, as the Dutch settlers call it, of the inn, on the seat near me, a mass of black mud, or some such substance. Always curious—a phrenologic doctor told me I had the bump of wonder—I took hold of it, and found it to be adherent. It smelt strongly of bitumen. The landlord seeing me examining it chimed in, and said that the Indians had brought it to him from thirteen miles beyond Cornwall's Creek, where there was an immense deposit of the same kind. It was, in fact, soft asphalte, or petroleum, or bitumen, or whatever the learned may please to designate it, in a state of coherence.

My researches did not stop here: I had had specimens of all the Canadian woods to send officially for transmission to England, and amongst others I had observed a very curious one, called white wood, which was certainly neither pine, nor any thing approaching to the fir kind. It was very light, very tenacious, and is extensively employed in this portion of Canada, where fir and pine are not common, for the purposes of flooring and building, making an extremely delicate and ornamental board.

In travelling along I had asked the name of every strange tree, and so frequently had received the words white wood for answer, that I at last found it was a Canadian poplar, which grows in the western and London districts to an enormous size.

The cotton wood is also another species of western poplar, and both would form a useful and an ornamental addition to our park scenery at home.

The white wood, the cotton wood, and the yellow white wood, are used in this part of Canada for all building purposes, wherein pine is employed elsewhere, and the last named makes the best flooring. I should think, from its lightness and beauty, that it might be used with great advantage in Tunbridge ware.

The quaking asp is also another poplar of western West Canada, and is a variety of the aspen.

Here too I began to observe gigantic walnut-trees, from which such a large proportion of household furniture throughout Canada is manufactured, but regretted to find that it is much wasted in being split up into rails for fences by the farmers, on account of its durability. They are, however, beginning to be sensible of its value, for it is now largely exported to England and elsewhere. The size of the black walnut and of the cotton wood is inconceivable: of the latter curbs for the mouths of large wells are often made, by merely hollowing out the trunk.

Vegetation in the western district is, in fact, extraordinary, and altogether it is undoubtedly the garden of Canada. Tobacco grows well in some portions of it, and is largely cultivated near the shores of Lake Erie. I believe most of the Havana cigars smoked in Canada, particularly at Montreal, are Canadian tobacco. So much the better; for if a man must put an enemy to his digestive organs into his mouth, it is better that that enemy should be the produce of the soil of which he is a native or denizen, as he derives some benefit from the consumption, although consumption of another sort may accrue.

I have long and earnestly thought upon the subject of the weed, and have come to the conclusion that, as a necessary of life, it is about upon a par with opium. Men of the lower classes, I mean labouring people, who leave off drinking either from religious motives or from fear, usually take to smoking, and in general their constitutions are as much injured by the one as by the other. Cigar-smoking is a sort of devil-may-care imitation of the vulgar by gentlemen, and is no more requisite for health or amusement than whiskey, dice, or cards. It is amusing in the extreme to see old fellows aping extreme juvenility, and professing to smoke before breakfast; and it is ridiculous to see young gentlemen, very young and very green, cigar in mouth, fancying it very manly and very independent to imitate a rough, weather-beaten sailor or soldier, who, not being able to smoke a cigar, sticks to the pipe. That it stupifies is certain, that it is very vulgar is more certain, and that it injures health is more certain still. I wonder if Father Matthew smokes—almost all priests do: they have very little other solace.

The approach to Chatham is very pretty. Young Thames, for I do not see why there should not be Young Thames as well as Young England, that most absurd of all D'Israelisms, looks enchanting in a country where lakes as flat on their shores as a pancake take the lead, and where rivers are creeks, and creeks are—nothing.

We crossed a long whitewashed bridge, much out of repair, and saw an enormous American flag upon a very little American schooner, which had penetrated thus far into the bowels of the land. Bunting cannot be dear in the United States, and English Manchester must drive a pretty good trade in this article.

The town of Chatham is situated on the banks of the Thames and of a large creek; and, being a Kentish man, I should have felt quite at home but for three things, videlicet, that enormous American flag; the name of the creek, which was Mac Gill or Mac something; and a thermometer pointing to somewhere about 101° Fahrenheit at nine a.m. Besides this, the town is a wooden one, and has a wooden little fort, which divides Scotland from Kent, or the river from the creek, nicely picketed in, and kept in the most perfect order by a worthy barrack serjeant, its sole tenant, whose room was hung round with prints of the Queen, Windsor Castle, the Duke of Wellington, and Lord Nelson—all in frames, and excellently well engraved, from the "Albion" newspaper.

The Albion newspaper is no ordinary hebdomadal; it has disseminated loyalty throughout America for years, and, as a gift on each 1st of January, has been in the habit of publishing a print of large size, engraved in exceedingly brilliant style, which is presented to its subscribers. The Queen, the Duke, the Conqueror of the Seas, Walter Scott, and his Monument at Edinburgh, &c., are the fruits; and these plates would sell in England for at least half a guinea, or a guinea each.

The Albion, moreover, gives extracts at length from the current literature of England; and thus science, art, politics, agriculture, find admirers and readers in every corner of the backwoods.

Dr. Bartlett, its editor, at New York, deserves much more than this ephemeral encomium, for he has done more than all the orators upon loyalty in the Canadas towards keeping up a true British spirit in it. The Albion, in fact, in Canada is a Times as far as influence and sound feeling go; and although, like that autocrat of newspapers, it differs often from the powers that be, John Bull's, Paddy's, and Sawney's real interests are at the bottom, and the bottom is based upon the imperishable rock of real liberty. It steers a medium course between the extrême droit of the so-called Family Compact, and the extrême gauche of the Baldwin opposition.

Political feeling ran very high in the section of country through which we are travelling, both in the war of 1812 and in the rebellion of 1837; and, from the vicinity of the Western district to the United States, in both instances it was inferred by the American people that an easy conquest was certain. Proclamations followed upon proclamations, and attacks upon attacks, but the people loved their soil, and the invaders were driven back. So it will be again, if, unhappily, war should follow the mad courses now pursuing. The Canadians at heart are sound, and nowhere is this soundness more apparent than in the western district. It is not the mere name of liberty which can tempt thinking men to abandon the reality.

It has fallen to my lot to be acquainted with many leaders of faction, both in the Old and in the New World, and I never yet knew one whose personal ambition or whose private hatred had not stimulated him to endeavour to overturn all order, all rule. The patriot, whose sole aim is to amend and not to destroy, is now-a-days a rara avis, particularly if he is needy. One has only to read with attention the details of the horrors of the French revolution to be fully impressed with this fact. Where was patriotism then? and was not Napoleon the real patriot when he said, "two or three six-pounders would have settled the canaille of Paris!" I by no means advocate the ultima ratio regum being resorted to in popular commotions, in saying this; but France would have been happier had the little corporal been permitted to use his artillerymen. It has often surprised me, in reading the history of the American revolution, assisted as the Americans were by the demoralised French of that day, that that revolution was so bloodless a one; a fact only to be accounted for by the agricultural and pastoral character of the people who engaged in it, and by the unwillingness, even at the last moment, to sever all ties between the parent and the child. The character of that population has greatly altered since; generations have been born on the soil, whose recollections of their progenitors across the Atlantic have dwindled to the smallest span; and the intermixture of races has since done everything but destroy all filial feeling, has in fact destroyed nearly all but the common language, whilst ultra-democracy has been steadily at work upon the young idea to inculcate hatred to monarchy, and, above all, to the limited monarchy of England. Will the result be less harmless than the Tea Triumph? The world, it is to be feared, will yet see two nations, the most free in the world, speaking the same tongue, educated from the same sources, embruing their hands in each other's blood, to build up a new universal system, impossible in its very nature, or to support that which the experience of ages has perfected, and which three estates so continually watch over each other to guard.

CHAPTER XIV.

Intense Heat—Pigs, the Scavengers of Canada—Dutch Country—Moravian Indians—Young Father Thames—Ague, a cure for Consumption—Wild Horses—Immense Marsh.

I never remember so hot a day as the 13th of July; people in England can have no idea of the heat in Canada, which they always figure to themselves as an hyperborean region. On our journey from Thamesville, when near Louisville, a neat hamlet by the wayside, in a beautiful country, settled by old Dutch families, on a fine bend of the Thames, we passed in the woods a dead horse, and found some friends at Chatham, who told us that it had dropped down from the intense heat. Those scavengers of Canada, the pigs, were like certain politic worms already busily at work on the carcase, in which indeed one had buried itself.

In this Dutch country, you find the new road to Lake Erie, to the Rondeau from Chatham graded, or ready for planking, for twenty-six miles, and the new road to Windsor is also nearly finished; so that Chatham will now have an excellent land route to the Detroit river, as well as to Lake Erie; and as the Rondeau, a remarkable round littoral lake, is also converting into an excellent harbour, all this portion of Canada, the fairest as well as the most fertile, will progress amazingly.

I saw the chief of the Moravian Indians near Thamesville, and had some conversation with him. He is a modest, middle-aged man, and rules over about two hundred and fifty well-behaved people. The government have given him two hundred acres of land in sight of the Moravian village, and there he dwells in patriarchal simplicity.

Their spiritual and temporal concerns are under the supervision of the brethren at Bethlehem, the principal settlement of the Moravian fraternity in the United States; and they have a neat chapel and school, conducted with the decorum and good results for which that sect are noted.

Petrolean springs and mineral oil fountains are frequent near this village, and the whole country here appears bituminous, the bed of the Thames being composed of shales highly impregnated with it. Salt is manufactured in small quantities by the Indians from brine-springs here.

We saw the remarkable harvest of 1845 in all its glory on this route, as the Dutch farmers were every where at this early period cutting the wheat, and heard that on Willett's farm on the Thames it had been cut as early as the 10th of July.

My compagnon de voyage I had taken up in the morning, on account of the intelligence which he displayed, and in return for the ride he gave me much information.

The banks of Young Father Thames, after leaving Chatham, and about it, are very low and flat, consequently, fever and ague are by no means rare visitors. He described the ague as being beyond a common Canada one; and, as he was of Yankee origin, the reader will readily understand his description of it. I asked him if he had ever had it. "Had it, I guess I have; I had it last fall, and it would have taken three fellows with such a fit as mine was to have made a shadow; why, my nose and ears were isinglass, and I shook the bedposts out of the perpendicular."

I queried whether the country was subject to any other diseases, such as consumption.

"If you have any friend with a consumption," said he, "send him to Thamesville; consumption would walk off slick as soon as he got the ague. No disorder is guilty of coming on before it, and it leaves none behind."

We left Chatham in the steamboat Brothers for Windsor at three o'clock p.m., after having had a very good dinner at Captain Ebbert's inn, the Royal Exchange, which would do credit to any town.

The Thames rolls for some miles, broad and deep, through a succession of corn-fields and meadows, with fine settlements, and, after passing through the great western marshes, enters Lake St. Clair, at twenty miles from Chatham. The rest of the route is across the lake by its southern shore, twenty miles more, and into the Detroit river for eleven miles to Windsor, on the Canada shore, and the city of Detroit, on the American side.

The Thames keeps up its English character well, for it passes through the townships of Chatham, Dover, Harwich, Raleigh, and Tilbury, before it reaches Lake St. Clair, and then we coast Rochester, Maidstone, and Sandwich.

The most curious thing on this route is the sinuosity of the river and the immense marsh, where the grasses are so luxuriant, that its appearance is that of the Pampas of South America, or of one unbroken sea of verdure. Nor is the grass, in its luxuriance, the only reminiscence of those vast meadows. Three hundred thousand acres, wholly unreclaimed on both sides of the river, are filled, particularly on the south side, with droves of wild horses and cattle—the former so numerous, that strings of them may be seen as far as the eye can reach; nor can you see the whole even near you from the deck of the vessel, as the grass is so high that sometimes they are hidden, and frequently you observe only their backs. They live here both in summer and in winter, but in very severe weather are said to go ashore, or into the higher lands, in search of the bark of the red elm. The owners brand them on the shoulder, and they are caught, when any are wanted, by snaring them with a noose.

These horses are small, and usually dark-coloured; and a good one is valued at fifty dollars, or twelve pounds ten shillings currency, about ten pounds English money. Hardy, patient, and excellent little animals they are.

I thought of the worthy lieutenant-governor of Upper Canada, Sir Francis Bond Head, when these wild horses of Canada first met my sight, as I saw, on a small scale, that which he has so vividly represented on so splendid a one in South America.

It is said that this immense prairie may be drained by lowering the St. Clair Lake, and some attempts have been ineffectually made to cultivate small portions of it near the mouth of the river, where there is a lighthouse. There were two huts, and people residing in them, with small garden patches of potatoes and peas. Forty acres had been ploughed by a settler, Mr. Thompson, of Chatham; but, although the soil is excellent, such is the vigorous growth of the grass, and the difficulty of getting rid of its roots, that it soon recovered its ancient domain. In fact, the wind spreads the seed rapidly; and as the kind is chiefly the blue-joint, it is almost impossible ever to get rid of it, unless the water-level is lowered, which is not very probable at present.

CHAPTER XV.

Why Engineer-officers have little leisure for Book-making—Caution against iced water—Lake St. Clair in a Thunderstorm—A Steaming Dinner—Detroit river and town—Windsor—Sandwich—Yankee Driver—Amherstburgh—French Canadian Politeness—Courtesy not costly—Good effects of the practice of it illustrated—Naked Indians—Origin of the Indians derived from Asia—Piratical attempt and Monument at Amherstburgh—Canadians not disposed to turn Yankees—Present state of public opinion in those Provinces—Policy of the Government—Loyalty of the People.

A person employed actively in public life is a very bad hand to engage in book-making. I often wonder whether this trifle, now intended as an offering to the reading people, will ever get into print. A little memorandum-book supplies the matériel, and a tolerable memory the embellishment. An engineer-officer, of all other functionaries, needs a memory; settling at one moment the expenditure of vast sums; at another, looking into the merits of a barrack damage worth sixpence; then, field-officer of the day inspecting guards—next, making experiments on the destructive effects of gunpowder, commencing with a percussion-pistol, and ending with a mine; buying land, taking altitudes of the sun and of the moon, examining a Gunter's chain or a theodolite, sitting as member of a court-martial, or of a board of respective officers, or counting the gold and silver in the military chest; superintending a fortification of the most intricate Vaubanism; regulating the dip of the needle, or the density of the earth; putting an awkward squad through the most approved manœuvres; studying the integral calculus, or the catenarian curve; bothered by Newton or La Place; reading German or Spanish; exploring Oregon, or any other terra incognita; building docks, supervising railways, surveying Ireland, governing a colony, conducting a siege, leading a forlorn hope; an Indian chief, or commanding an army (both the latter rather rare); well may his motto be, as that of his corps is, Ubique. So, gentle reader, if there is wandering in the matter of these pages, put it down, not to the want of method or manners, but to the want of time; for, even in a dull Canadian winter, it is only by fits and snatches that the mysteries of book-making can be practised. The intervals are uncertain, the opportunities few. At one hour, one is drawing one's sword; at the next, in

The manner in which Indian rights are treated in America is so glaring, that the philanthropist shudders. Protocols pass; the country west of the Mississippi is declared to belong first to Mexico, then to Spain, then to France, then to England, then to the United States. At last, the United States, strong enough to play a new game, a much more lofty one than the Tea Tragedy, defies the whole world, issues a decree irrevocable as those famous ones of the Medes and the Persians, and, perhaps, equally to pass into oblivion, that all the New World is to be the property of the descendants of the Anglo-Saxons—all the New World, never mind whether it be Monarchical England's, Imperial Brazil, Republican Mexico, Peru, Bolivia, &c.—all is to be guided by the banner of the Stars and Stripes.

Who among the statesmen ever dreams that the Red Man has any rights, who ever cares about his property in the wilds of the Prairies, of the Rocky Mountains, of the unknown lands of the Pacific! The United States declares that all Northern America is hers from the Atlantic to the Pacific, and the bloody flag of war is unfurled to obtain the commencement of this crusade against right and against reason, although the United States has ten times as much land already as ten times its present population can fill or cultivate, and then, Oregon is the war cry,

"Truly to speak it, and with no addition,

We go to gain a little patch of ground,

That hath in it no profit but the name;

To pay five dollars, five, I would not farm it;

Two thousand souls and twenty million dollars

Will not debate the question of this straw;

This is th' imposthume of much wealth and peace,

That inward breaks, and shows no cause without

Why the man dies—"

and then, in case Oregon should fail, advantage is taken of Mexico's distractions to negotiate for California.

The Red Man, the poor Red Man, may however have a voice in all this, that may speak in thunder. He is neither so powerless, nor so utterly contemptible as is supposed. In the wilds of the West, it is said, including the roaming horsemen of Mexico, 100,000 warriors exist. Even against 20,000, what army entangled in the forest, hidden in the Prairie grass, lost in the wilderness defiles of the vast Andes of the north, could also exist? and can the American government afford to detach regular troops for such a dreadful warfare? will the militia undertake it? Can an American fleet

She said nothing, but, returning to the kitchen, which is the common reception-room in country places, put a few eggs into the pot over the fire, and got the tea-pot. I saw several fine hams hanging to the rafters, so I took one down, got a knife, and was about to cut some slices to broil, when she stopped me. "You haven't got the best," says the old dame; "I shall cut you one myself." And so she did, spread the cloth, set two tea-cups, &c., and a capital supper we had, for a fine fowl was spitchcocked.

After supper, Mother Craig asked me to smoke another pipe with her and her good man, who was lame and unable to work, and some of her sons, &c. came in from the fields. I missed her soon afterwards; but, after a quarter of an hour, she came in again, whispered that she wanted me, and I followed her. "It is time," said the dame, "for you to go to bed; for you must be up by candlelight to-morrow morning, as your journey is a long one; see if this will do." In an inner chamber were two beds; one a feather bed, the other a pine-branch one, with clean blankets, snow-white sheets, a night-cap of the best, water, &c. "That's your bed," said Mrs. Craig; "the other is for the colonel, as you call him. Good night; I will call you in the morning—take care, and put your candle out." I laughed in my sleeve, went out, called the colonel, who would have been otherwise left in the dark, for the family soon retired for the night, and I need not say gave him the best bed, as he thought; the best, however, I kept myself, for a bed of fresh pine shoots to a weary traveller in Canada is better than all the feather beds in the world, particularly in the New World.

So much for life in the Bush; and I was then not quite so old as at present; but, even in youth, experience had taught me the utility of taking the world easy. My friend the colonel, next morning, after a sound sleep, said, "Whenever I am obliged to travel in the Bush, I wish you may be with me;" and old mother Craig, who is now no longer in this world, thought the next morning, as she afterwards said, that, after all, the colonel was not so bad as she had imagined.

This is, for one may as well deprecate a little in talking about fastidiousness, not told by way of evincing superior knowledge of the world, but just to show you, gentle or simple reader, whichever you may be, that, in a sentimental journey through Canada, you must accommodate yourself a little to the manners and customs of the population, if you expect to get along quietly, and to form any just opinion of the country.

When we saw the naked Indians under the wide-spreading trees, literally taking their ease, sub tegmine fagi, I thought that, if a Cockney could be transported in a balloon from Temple Bar right down here, what a barbarous land he would say Canada was, and his note-book would run thus: "Landed on the banks of a river twice as broad as the Thames, and saw the inhabitants burnt brown, and stark naked, under the trees. Oh, fie!"

Really, however, there is nothing very startling in seeing a naked Indian, whether it is that the bronze colour of his red skin looks so artificial, or that white flesh is so rarely observed, except in fashionable ball-rooms, I do not know; but I do know that I should most unequivocally feel queer, if I suddenly saw twenty or thirty naked Cockneys squatting and smoking under the trees on the banks of the Serpentine River, even if the thermometer was at 110° at the moment. Such is custom. A naked Indian looks natural, and a naked Cockney would look contra bonos mores, to say the least of it.

The Indian, whether dressed or undressed, is a modest man—not so always the Cockney; and there is an air of grandeur and natural freedom about the savage, which civilized man wants, or which modern coats, waistcoats, trowsers, and hats, are unquestionably not calculated to inspire.

Look at the statue of a Roman Consul, or at Apollo Belvidere, in his scanty clothing, and then you will understand what I mean; or, what is better, look at your grandmother's picture, with her hair powdered, stomacher, and farthingale, and then at the Venus de Medicis, and you will know better, if you are a man of taste. How the American ladies, who do not admit such words as naked or legs into their vocabulary, there being an especial act of Congress forbidding females to use them, get over the difficulty of Indians in their war costume, has puzzled me not a little. To draw a curtain before an Indian chief would be rather a venturous affair, as he is a little sensitive; and, when well painted, thinks himself extremely comme il faut, and very well dressed. But de gustibus non est disputandum, and so forth.

It is a queer country, this Amherstburgh country: French Canadians as primitive as Père Adam and Mère Eve; Indians of the old stock and of the new stock, that is to say, very few of the former, but a good many of the latter; owning both to French and to British half parentage; negroes in abundance; runaway slaves and their descendants, a mixture of all three; and plenty of loafers from the United States. In fact, it would seem as though Shem, Ham, and Japhet, had all representatives here, for Europeans and Americans of every possible caste are exhibited along this frontier, only I did not either see or hear of an Israelite; but some antiquarians contend that the Indians are a portion of the lost tribes. Their Asiatic origin is more decided. The feather of an eagle stuck in the warrior's hair is nothing more than the peacock's plume in a Tartar's bonnet. Then there is the patriarchal mode of government in the nations. Polybius says that the Carthaginians (Africans, by the way) scalped their enemies. The Kalmucks pluck out their beards, so do the Indians. The Pottawotamies, and most of the more savage one of the two drawing-rooms, namely, that where ladies congregate, and that in which steel-pens chiefly shine.

But it is necessary, nevertheless, to go on with any thing one seriously begins; and, although the "art and practique part" of book-making is, considering the requisite labour of bad penmanship, rather disgusting, yet the giving "a local habitation and a name" to the ideas floating on the sensorium is pleasant enough. It would be better if one had a steam-pen, for I always find my ideas much more rapid than consists with a goose quill. The unbending of the mind in a trifle like the present is also agreeable; and if the reader only likes it, as much as it amuses me and it whiles away graver cares, and the every-day monotony of a matter-of-fact existence, so much the better. An engineer-officer has no time to become a blasé, but every body else is not in his position, and thus this "little boke" may be taken up with the morning paper, and your man of the world may be induced to go so far as to say, "Wild horses in Canada! I never heard of them before; I will positively read a page or two more some rainy morning."

Blasé, dear blasé, if ever you should muster up courage to go to Canada for relief, and want to see the wild horses, pray do not go towards the end of July; and if you do, don't drink iced water on board the Brothers, with the thermometer at 100° Fahrenheit, as I did, from very exhaustion. An old farmer on board cautioned me, but I was proud and thirsty, and did the deed. Sorely was it repented of; for, when we landed at night, I was seized with a violent pain in the heart region, accompanied by great uneasiness and lassitude; and, it was not until after lying down quietly for several hours that the symptoms abated. I was, however, very well the next day, but will not drink iced water in the dog-days any more in Canada West. Yet the Yankees do it with impunity.

We entered Lake St. Clair in a thunderstorm at half-past five, but, fortunately for us, in this shallow lake, averaging only three fathoms or eighteen feet in depth, the storm, which in other places was a tornado, did nothing but frighten us at a distance.

It tore large trees up by the roots, and unroofed houses not many miles off; and, had it caught us with so much top-hamper as the steamboat had, perhaps we should have sounded the lake in propriá personá, without being witnesses as to its actual mysteries afterwards.

We steamed on, however, near the south shore for twenty miles, and entered the Detroit, or Narrow St. Lawrence, before the light of day had vanished, observing islands, &c., and arrived safely at Windsor, at Iron's Inn, at ten p.m., having experienced the pleasures of an adverse gale and intense heat.

The dinner on board was by no means a luxury, for, although very good, the company was numerous, the cabin near the boiler, all the dishes smoking, the room low and small, and the thermometer as aforesaid on deck, so that we literally were steaming, for it must have been close to the boiling point.

Thursday morning, the 14th of July, was as hot as ever; and if I could, I would not have crossed over to the United States, where the famous city of Detroit stared me in the face on the other side of the river, about as broad as the Thames just below bridge.

It was, like all recent American cities, very staring and very juvenile, with large piles of brick buildings scattered amidst white painted wooden ones, and covered an immense space, with many churches, looking very fine at a distance, an immense crowd of very large, bright, white, and green, coarsely painted and loosely built steam-vessels at the wharfs, and small, dirty, steam ferry-boats, constantly plying to and from the British shore.

Windsor is a small village, scattered, as most Canadian villages are, with a little barrack, in which a detachment of the Royal Canadian Rifle corps is stationed, to watch the frontier. The Americans are now building a large fort on the opposite side.

I left Windsor at nine a.m., in a light waggon and pair, and rolled along the bank of the river to Sandwich, the county or district town, two miles from Windsor, opposite to which the Americans are building a fortification of some size, but apparently only an extensive earth-work.

It is a very pleasant drive along the banks of the Straitened River, or Detroit, close to the water, and occasionally in it, to refresh the horses. The population, chiefly French Canadians and Indians, occupy the roadside in detached farms; the Canadian huts and houses being, as in Lower Canada, invariably whitewashed and planted at short intervals.

We saw the Indians both industrious and idle: some were hoeing maize, others harvesting wheat, and the habitants were also very busy in the fields.

The idle Indians, the most numerous, were lounging along the banks, under the shade of melancholy boughs, as naked as they were born, bathing, smoking, or making baskets. In the intense heat I envied them, and thought of the days of Paradise when tailors were not.

We stopped in this intense heat at Maître Samondon's tavern, having passed Sandwich, which has church, chapel, jail, and court-house, and is plentifully inhabited by French, whose domiciles evidently date from its first settlement. I saw some of the largest pear-trees here that I had ever seen; they were as big as good-sized walnut-trees in England.

We had a Yankee driver, a young fellow, whose ease and good-temper amused me very much. He had good horses, drove well, and had been in his time all sorts of things; the last trade, that of a mail-driver on the opposite shores, where, he said, the republic were going ahead fast, for they were copying Europeans, and had taken to robbing the mail by way of raising the wind; so that, in some place he mentioned in Pennsylvania, it was a service of danger to drive, for they fired out of the Bush and killed the horses occasionally. He told us several feats of his own against these robbers, but concluded by guessing that he should not have to carry a six-barrel Colt's revolver in Canaday; for "them French" never robbed mails.

He drove us to Amherstburgh, through a rich and beautiful grain country, in four hours, eighteen miles, and we stopped an hour at Samondon's, where nothing but French was spoken, and a long discourse held upon the crops and the state of the country. As I had an orderly with me, and as red coats had not been seen in that part of the world since the rebellion, we caused some emotion and conversation on the road. A very old, garrulous French Canadian, who was smoking his pipe in the "kitchen and parlour and hall," came and sat by me, and, after beating about the bush a long time with all the "politesse possible," at length asked me who I was, and if the army was coming back among them. I told him who I was, a lieutenant-colonel of engineers; and the old Jean Jacques, after looking at me a minute or so, got up and fetched a small glass of whiskey and water, and with the best grace in the world presented it, with a cigar, taking another of both himself, and, touching his glass to mine in true French style, bowed and said, "A votre santé, mon colonel; you have got a devilish good place of it!" The French Canadians on the Detroit river were all loyal during the rebellion, and this old farmer was a sample of them.

When the horses were fed, and I had, as is customary, treated the driver, we departed amidst the pleasing sounds of Bien obligé, bon voyage. If they had cheated me, I should have been content, so much is politeness worth; and the Canadian French peasant is a primitive being, and as polite as a baron of the ancien régime. It was quite refreshing in such hot weather to meet with a little civilization, after being occasionally witness to the reverse from the newest people in the world. Il coute si peu.

How shocking, a sensitive parvenu will say, to sit down in a common kitchen, and drink a glass of whiskey and water with peasants! It puts me in mind of a very fine young lady, whose grandfather had been a butcher, and her father none of the richest; who, being met in the streets with some threadpapers or small package of lace in her hand early on a cold day, said, to a gentleman who stopped to ask her how she did, "I am very well, I thank you; but this parcel makes my hand so cold!" Or, for a still finer illustration,

I knew a nouvelle riche who, not being addressed by a tradesman in a little town in his bill by a factitious title, to which she imagined that she had a right, sent back his letter open to the post-office, with an intimation to the postmaster that letters so improperly addressed would not be received.

I have always perceived that a fuss about family and noble connections betrays either that the fuss-maker is naturally a vulgar soul, or that it is deemed necessary, from an excess of weakness, to support a position of an equivocal nature. A gentleman never derogates from his true position, let him be placed in whatever circumstances he may; and an over-fastidious traveller, or a pretender to great importance in a new country, is the most foolish of all foolish folks.

I remember travelling once in the wild Bush with a person, who, from long-established military habits of command, thought that he could order everything as he liked. We were benighted at a farm-house, where the old lady proprietress eked out her livelihood by receiving casual visitors, but disdained the thought of "keeping tavern," as it is called, in the backwoods of Canada West. He ordered, rather peremptorily, supper and beds for two—it would have been better that he had ordered pistols and coffee for the same number, for then the dame would have looked upon him as simply mad. No notice whatever was taken of his demands, but I saw her choler rising; fortunately, I knew her character. We were many miles from any habitation: and the horses jaded out as well as ourselves; so I took no notice either; but, observing the dame take her seat in the old-fashioned ample chimney, I took another opposite to her, and, observing her commence lighting her pipe, asked her for one, and we puffed out volumes of smoke—those were my smoking days—for a long time at each other in perfect silence. At last, I broke the ice.

"Mrs. Craig, your tobacco is bad; next time I come by, I will bring you some excellent."—A gracious nod!—We smoked on, and every now and then she condescended to speak upon indifferent subjects. At last, she got up and went into another room. I followed her; for I saw she wanted to speak to me without my friend.—"Who is that man?" quoth the dame.—"Colonel So and so," responded I.—"I don't care whether he be a colonel or a general; all I can say is, that he has got no manners; and the devil a supper or a bed shall he get here!"—"Oh, my good lady," said I, "he is not used to travel in the Bush, and is a stranger, and not over-young, as you see; besides, he is regularly tired out. Let me give him half my supper, and perhaps he can sleep in the chimney-corner. I don't care about a bed myself; pine branches will do for me, and an old buffalo robe, which I have in the waggon."

a small portion of the press, and by disappointed speculators in politics—men who have lost high offices, for which they were never fitted, either by capacity or connection with the best interests of the people, and who allied themselves to the French Canadian party merely to accomplish their own ends.

The real substance, or, as Cobbett called it, the bone and marrow of Canada, is not composed of needy politicians or of reckless adventurers, caring not whether they plunge their adopted country into all the horrors of revolution or of anarchy.

A man possessing a few hundred acres of land, with every comfort about him, paying no taxes but those for the improvement of his property, feeling the government rein only as a salutary check to lawlessness, and looking stedfastly abroad, is not very likely, for abstract notions of right and equality, to sacrifice reality, or to suppose that Mr. Baldwin, amiable as he is, is infallible: whilst Mr. Baldwin himself, the ostensible, but not the real leader of the out-and-out reformers, will pause before he even dreams of alienating the country in which he, from being a very poor man originally, has, through the industry and talent of his father, and a fortuitous train of circumstances, connected with the rise and progress of the city of Toronto, and the rise of the price of land as Canada advances in population and wealth, become a great land-holder.

I have no idea that this Corypheus of Canadian reform has the most remote idea of annexing Canada to the United States, or that he is mentally fighting for anything more than an Utopia similar to that of O'Connell in Ireland. In short, the grand struggle of the radical reform party of Upper Canada has been, and for which they joined the French Canadian party, to have a repeal of the union as far as control over the provincial funds and offices exists, on the side of England.

They would have no objection to see a British prince on the Canadian throne, or a British viceroy sitting at the council board of Montreal, but they want to be governed without the intervention of the colonial office; and perhaps, rather than not have the loaves and fishes at their own entire disposal, they would in the end go so far as to desire entire separation from the Mother Country, and seek the armed protection of that enormous power which is so rapidly rising into notice on their borders.

But then they calculate—for there is a good sprinkling of Jonathanism in their ranks—that that enormous power is grasping at too much already, defying the whole world, and seeking to establish a perfectly despotic dominion itself over the whole continent which Columbus and Cabot discovered, and not excluding the archipelago of the Western Indies.

They live too near the littorale of the Republic, or rather the democracy of America, not to see hourly the effects of Lynch law and mob rule; and, however some of the most daring or reckless among them may occasionally employ that very mob rule to intimidate and carry elections, they very well know that the peaceable inhabitants of both Canadas are too respectable and too numerous to permit such courses to arrive at a head. Once rouse the yeomanry of Canada West, and their energies would soon manifest themselves in truly British honesty and British feeling. John Bull is not enamoured of the tender mercies of canallers and loafers, and the French Canadian peasantry and small farmers are innocent of the desire to imitate the heroes of Poissardism.

No person in public life can judge better of the feelings of the people as a mass, in Canada, than those who have commanded large bodies of the militia. Put the query to any officer in the army who has had such a charge, and the universal answer will be: "The militia of Canada are loyal to Britain, without vapouring or boasting of that loyalty; for they are not by natural constitution a very speaking race, or given at every moment to magnify; but they will fight, should need be, for Victoria, her crown, and dignity."

It may be said that an officer in the army is not the best judge of the feelings of the people, as they would not express them in his presence; but when an officer has been intimately mingled with them by such events as those of the troubles of 1837 and 1838, and has so long known the country, the case is altered; he comes to have a personal as well as a general knowledge of all ranks, degrees, and classes, and can weigh the ultimate objects of popular expression. I have no hesitation in saying, possessed as I have been of this knowledge, that the people of Canada have not a desire to become independent now, any more than they have a desire to be annexed to and fraternize with the United States.

Many years ago, on my first visit to Canada, in 1826, when such a thing as expressions of disloyalty was almost unknown, and long before Mackenzie's folly, I remember being struck with the speech at a private dinner party of a person who has since held high office, respecting the independence of Canada: he observed that it must ultimately be brought about. The colony then was in its mere infancy, and this person no doubt had dreams of glory, although in outward life he was one of the most uncompromising of the colonial ultra-tories.

Just before the rebellion broke out, I was conversing with another person, now no more, of a similar stamp, but possessing much more influence, who began to be alarmed for his extensive lands, all of which he had obtained by grants from the Crown, and he feared that the time specified by the first-mentioned person had arrived. His observations to me were revelations of an astounding nature; for he thought that we were too near a republic to continue long under a monarchy, and that, in fact, absurd titles, such as those borne by the then governor, Sir Francis Head, alluding to his being merely a knight bachelor, were likely to create contempt in Canada, instead of affection. My friend, who, like the first-mentioned, was rather weak, although acute enough when self-interest was concerned, was evidently casting about in his mind's eye for a new order of things, in which to secure his property and his official influence.

Lord Sydenham and Lord Durham saw and knew a great deal of this vacillation among all parties in Canada. They saw that the great game of the leaders was office, office, office; and when Lord Metcalfe had had sufficient time to discover the real state of the country, he saw it too. Hence arose the absolute necessity for removing the seat of government from Toronto to Kingston. The ultra-tories were just as troublesome as the ultra-levellers, and it was requisite to neutralize both, by getting out of the sphere of their hourly influence. The inhabitants of Kingston, a naval and military town, whose revenues had been chiefly derived from those sources, were loyal, without considering it of the utmost consequence that their loyalty should form the basis of every government, or that the governor was not to open his mouth, or use his pen, unless by permission. They were the true medium party.

Then arose the desire to do justice to the Gallo-Canadians, who had before been wholly neglected, and looked upon as too insignificant to have any voice in public affairs, whilst they were mistrusted also, owing to the Papineau demonstration.

The British government, superior to all these petty colonial interests, saw at once that to ensure loyalty it was only proper to administer justice impartially to all creeds and to all classes, and that the French Canadians, whose numbers were at least equal to the British Canadians, had a positive right to be heard and a positive claim to be equitably treated.

There was no actual innate desire in the Canadian mind to shake off the British domination for that of the democracy of the United States. An absurd notion had gathered strength in 1837 that they were at last powerful enough to set up for themselves, to constitute la Nation Canadienne, forgetting that Great Britain could swallow them up at a mouthful, and that the Americans would, if John Bull did not. The proclamation of General Nelson or Brown, or some such patriot, set the affair in its true point of view. No longer any religion was to be predominant; the feudal laws were to be abolished; and the celebrated ninety-two resolutions, which had cost Papineau and his legion so much care and anxiety, were swept away as if they were dust. A Jack Cade had started up, whose laws were to be administered at the point of the bayonet.

The eyes of the leading French Canadians, gentlemen of education, were soon opened, and the vision of glory evaporated into thin air. But still they felt themselves oppressed, they enjoyed not the coveted rights of subjects of England; and accordingly the successive governments of Lord Durham, Lord Sydenham, and Sir Charles Bagot were eras of political struggles to obtain it.

Lord Metcalfe had had experience in colonies of long standing, had been successful, bore the character of a just, patient, and decided man, and had wealth enough to cause his independence to be respected.

The fight for supremacy between the ultra-tory and ultra-radical parties became fiercer and more fierce, and it was dolefully augured that the province was lost to England, as he would not yield to the haughty demands of the first, nor to the threats and menaces of the latter.

When the Baldwin ministry was dismissed, even cautious people were heard to say, that new troubles were at hand; and the ultra-tories did not scruple to avow that the country was in danger, unless they were readmitted to power.

Placed between these belligerents, Lord Metcalfe, who kept his own counsel to the last secret and undivulged, steered a course which has hitherto worked well. He chose a medium party, and removed the seat of government to Montreal, not in the heart of French Canada, as it is supposed in England, but within a few miles of British Canada and close to the eastern townships, where a British population is dominant, whilst in the city itself British interests surpass all others; it being the heart and lungs of the Canadian mercantile world, whilst it has the advantage of easy steam communication with Quebec, the seat of military power, and with Upper Canada, both by the St. Lawrence and the Rideau Canals.

The French, no longer neglected and seeing the seat of government permanently located in their country, seeing also that they had been admitted to share power and office, have been tranquillized; and the result of the elections placed Lord Metcalfe comparatively at ease, and rendered the task of his successor less onerous. Had his health been spared, the blessing of his wise rule would long have been felt. He is deeply and universally regretted throughout Canada.

As a proof of the loyalty of the Canadians, it is right to mention that, whilst I am penning these pages, the press is teeming with calls to the volunteers and militia to sustain Britain in the Oregon war; and, because the militia is not prematurely called out, the administrator of the government is attacked on all sides. Whilst I am writing, the Hibernian Society, in an immense Roman Catholic procession, passes by. There are four banners. The first is St. Patrick, the second Queen Victoria, the third Father Matthew, the fourth the glorious Union flag. Reader, it is the 17th of March, St. Patrick's Day, and the band plays God save the Queen!

CHAPTER XVI.

The Thames Steamer—Torrid Night—"The Lady that helped" and her Stays—Port Stanley—Buffalo City— Its Commercial Prosperity— Newspaper Advertisements—Hatred to England and encouragement of Desertion—General Crispianus— Lake Erie in a rage—Benjamin Lett— Auburn Penitentiary— Crime and Vice in the Canadas—Independence of Servants—Penitentiaries unfit for juvenile offenders—Inefficiency of the Police—Insolence of Cabmen—Carters—English rule of the road reversed— Return to Toronto.

The heat at Amherstburgh was so desiccating, that I was glad to leave even my urbane host, serjeant-major as he had been of a royal regiment, and his crowded though clean and comfortable inn, for the spacious deck of the splendid Canadian steamer Thames, Captain Van Allan, on board of which was to be enjoyed the absolute luxury of a spacious state-room upon deck. Alas for the roomy state-room! even in its commodious berth, rest could not be enjoyed, for the night was a torrid one; nothing in the Western Indies could beat it, only there was no yellow fever, although plenty of yellow countenances presented themselves on the shoulders of Americans from the South, and coloured waiters; but that which actually at last put me in a fever was the sight of the female attendant of the ladies' cabin, whose form was so buckled up in stays of the most rigid order, that the heat, American-bred as she was, appeared to have rendered her a Niobe, for she was tall and as straight as a poplar-tree, and much of the colour of its inner rind. Oh! the heat, the intolerable heat, on Lake Erie that night! The worthy captain declared he had never experienced its like, and that as for rest it was impracticable. If the lady's-maid, or "the lady that helped" in the ladies' cabin, as she is called in American boats, kept her stays on that night, Heaven help her! She must have been in a greater state of despair than the man in armour on Lord Mayor's day, who requires to go to bed after a warm bath, the moment he takes his stays off.

But we steamed on, and the boilers themselves were not a whit hotter than we were. How the stokers stood it is a marvel to this day. I suffered dreadfully with the prickly heat, as if in the West Indies.

The Thames is the most splendid boat on Lake Erie, and that is saying a good deal; for the Americans have so many, and several so much larger than this Britisher, that it is a matter of surprise that she should beat them all in convenience, build, and speed; and yet, according to received opinion, the Yankee builders of vessels excel us "by a long chalk," to use a Yankee figure of speech. It is so, however, and is so acknowledged on both sides of the water, that the Thames, Captain Van Allan, takes the shine out of them all.

We started from Amherstburgh, where she called on her way from Detroit, and left Bullock's inn for the steamer which was close at hand, at nine o'clock p.m., and got under steam and travelled all night at a most rapid rate, nor stopped until eight a.m., the next morning, at Port Stanley, formerly called Kettle Creek, a small village with a fine parallel pier harbour, which, unlike Amherstburgh, has thriven amazingly during the past seven years, before which I recollect it to have consisted of about three or four houses. It is now a thriving village; and, as it has a planked road reaching far into the interior, is every day going ahead. The plank road leads to London, twenty-six miles distant. The piers of this artificial harbour are much too narrow, consequently it is dangerous to approach in stormy weather; and, as Lake Erie is a very turbulent little ocean, they must be modified some day or other, whenever the Board of Works is rich enough.

We took in several passengers here, mostly Americans touring, and the vessel was now full, for we had a large proportion of the same class from Detroit. They were chiefly people from the hotter regions of the States, and resembled each other remarkably; sallow, sharp-angled, acute-looking physiognomies: the men tall and loosely jointed; the women prematurely old, and not very handsome. They were quiet and respectable in their manners and demeanour; in fact, too quiet, contrasting strongly in this respect with the real, genuine Yankee.

We reached Buffalo at seven in the evening, after encountering a thunderstorm, which appeared to be very severe towards the shores of the American side of Lake Erie.

Such a mob as poured on board the vessel, after she had with much difficulty threaded the inconvenient, narrow, muddy creek on which Buffalo is located, I never beheld before: blacks and whites, browns and yellows, cabmen and carters, porters and tavern-scouts, pickpockets and free and enlightened citizens.

How the passengers got their baggage conveyed to their hotels, or dwellings, is beyond my art to imagine. Insolent and daring, if these be a pattern mob, Heaven defend us Britishers from democracy! for freedom reigns at Buffalo in a pattern of the newest, which the seldomer copied the better. But one must not judge the money-getting citizens of this fine town by the scenes in the Wapping part of it; for, if one did, it would necessarily be said that they were not an enviable race.

Buffalo, a mere wooden village, burnt during the war of 1812, is now a large and flourishing city, containing 30,000 inhabitants; and, if it had a good harbour, would soon rival New York. To prove this, I beg the reader to take the trouble to peruse the accompanying statement of the present commerce of that city, from the Buffalo Commercial Advertiser of January 10, 1846, by which it will be seen that in the year 1845 the increase of vessels trading with it was enormous, and that by the Welland Canal, or an American ship canal, round the Falls of Niagara, they already contemplate a direct trade with Europe in British bottoms.

"There has been a prodigious accession to the Lake marine during the past season—no less than sixty vessels, whose aggregate tonnage is over 13,000 tons, and at an outlay of 825,000 dollars. Had we not the evidence before us, the assertion would stagger belief.

"More than usual pains were taken by us, during the past season, to procure information on this head and others touching thereto, the result of which we now present in our annual list of new vessels. This season we have ventured beyond the immediate margin of Lake Erie, and those other broad lakes beyond, to Lake Ontario, a knowledge of whose marine is now deemed essential to a thorough understanding of our lake matters.

NUMBER, TONNAGE, AND ESTIMATED COST OF NEW VESSELS BUILT IN 1845, FROM THIS CITY WESTWARD TO CHICAGO.

Name.	Class.	Tons.	Where built.	Dollars.
Niagara	steamer	1,075	Buffalo	95,000
Oregon	...	781	Newport, Michigan	55,000
Boston	...	775	Detroit	55,000
Superior	...	567	Perrysburg, O.	45,000
Troy	...	547	Maumee City, O.	40,000
London	...	456	Chippewa, C. W.	46,000
Helen Strong	...	253	Monroe, Michigan	22,000
John Owen	...	205	Truago, do.	20,000
Romeo	...	180	Detroit, do.	12,000

Enterprise	...	100	Green Bay, W. T.	8,000
Empire, 2nd	steamer	100	Grand Rapids, Mic.	8,000
Algomah	...	100	St. Joseph River, do.	8,000
Pilot	...	80	Union City, do.	5,000
Princeton	propeller	456	Perrysburg, O.	40,000
Oregon	...	313	Cleveland, O.	18,000
Phœnix	...	305	ditto	22,000
Detroit	...	290	Detroit, Michigan	15,000
Odd Fellow	brig	225	Cleveland, O.	9,000
Enterprise	...	267	Grand Rapids, Mich.	8,000
Wing-and-wing	schooner	228	Cleveland, O.	9,000
Magnolia	...	200	Charlestown, O.	2,000
Scotland	...	300	Perrysburg, O.	8,000
J.Y. Seammon	...	134	Chicago, Ill.	8,000
Napoleon	...	250	Sault Ste Marie	8,000
Freeman	...	190	Charleston, O.	7,500
Eagle	...	180	Sandusky, O.	7,000
Bonesteel	...	150	Milwaukie, W. T.	6,000
Sheppardson	...	130	ditto	5,000
Rockwell	...	120	ditto	5,000
E. Henderson	...	110	ditto	4,500
Rainbow	...	117	Sheboygan	4,000
C. Howard	...	103	Huron, O.	4,000
J. Irwin	...	101	Cleveland, O.	4,000
Avenger	...	78	Cottesville, Michigan	3,000
Flying Dutchman	...	74	Madison, O.	4,000
Cadet	...	72	Cleveland, O.	3,500
W. A. Adair	...	61	ditto	3,000
Elbe	...	57	ditto	3,000
Planet	...	24	ditto	3,000
Albany	...	148	Raised and re-rigged	2,503
Pilot	...	50	Milwaukie, W. T.	2,500
Mary Anne	schooner	60	Milwaukie, W. T.	1,000
Marinda	...	60	Lexington, Michigan	3,000

Sparrow	...	50	Chora, ditto	2,500
Big B.	...	60	18 mile creek,	2,500
Hard Times	...	45	ditto	1,500
Friendship	sloop	45	Sheboygan, W. T.	2,000
Buffalo	...	30	New Buffalo, Mich.	1,000
		— — —		— — — —
Total, 48 vessels		10,207		659,000

"During the past season we stated that there was employed on the lakes a marine equal to 80,000 tons; we have assurance now that even that large estimate was below the reality. The latest returns to Congress, in 1843, gave 60,000 tons; but, as those documents are always a year or two behind the reality, and embrace dead as well as living vessels, they are of very little consequence. The existing and employed tonnage is what is most desired. The subjoined shows the number, class, tonnage, and cost of vessels built on this and the other upper lakes during the past five seasons. By adding the cost of annual repairs and money expended in enlarging and re-modelling vessels, the sum would reach 2,500,000 dollars. The total number of vessels built during that period is 179.

	Steamers	Prop'rs.	Sail.	Tons.	Dollars.
1845	13	4	32	10,207	659,000
1844	9	none	34	9,145	548,000
1843	6	4	23	4,880	336,000
1842	2	none	23	3,000	164,000
1841	1	none	28	3,530	173,000
	— —	— —	— —	— — —	— — — —
Total	31	8	140	30,302	1,880,000

"The whole of the above vessels were built above the Falls, at places between this port and Chicago, by capital drawn from the many sources legitimately pertaining to the lake business, and designed as a permanent investment. What has been done below Niagara, in the same field, during the past season, may be seen in the subjoined list of

VESSELS BUILT ON LAKE ONTARIO, 1845.

Syracuse	propeller	315	Oswego, N. Y.
H. Clay	...	300	Dexter, do.
Hampton	brig	300	Pt. Peninsula, do.
T. Wyman	...	258	Oswego, do.
Algomah	...	335	Cape Vincent, do.
Wabash	...	314	Sack. Harbour, do.
Crispin	...	151	ditto
Liverpool	...	350	Garden Is., C.W.
Quebec	brig	280	Long Island, C.W.
H. H. Sizer	schooner	242	Pillar Point, N.Y.
Maid of the Mill	...	200	Oswego, do.
Milan	...	147	Pt. Peninsula, do.
H. Wheaton	...	200	Oswego, do.
Welland	...	220	ditto
Josephine	...	175	ditto
	...	— — —	
Total 15 vessels,		3,787	tons.

"To which must be added the schooner J. S. Weeks, rebuilt and enlarged at Point Peninsula, at a heavy outlay; and also the schooner Georgiana Jenia, at St. Catharine's, which was cut in two, and rebuilt. The Josephine and Wyman are rebuilds, but so thoroughly as almost to fall within the denomination of new craft. The Wyman is polacca-rigged, the only one in service, we think. The Algomah is full rigged, and, like the others, very strongly built. The Quebec and Liverpool are also well ironed, and designed for Atlantic service, when the St. Lawrence locks will admit of a free passage.

"There have been built on the lower lake other vessels than those embraced in the above list, including some steamers; and, in order to give our exchanges an opportunity to present the entire number and amount of expense, we omit any estimate of the cost and general outlay of the vessels named above. Applying our data, however, we make the outlay 25,000 dollars each, for the two propellers, and 127,000 dollars for the fifteen sail vessels, being a total of 177,000 dollars.

"Of some sixty steamers now owned on the lake (Erie), there are required for the several lines, when the consolidation exists, about thirty boats. There are also used, at the same time, some ten more small boats, between intermediate ports, for towing, &c., to which we also add the London and four others, belonging to and owned in Canada. There are also fourteen propellers, and ten more to be added on the opening of navigation in the spring, with fifty brigs and two hundred and seventy schooners, known to be in commission, giving the annexed summary of lake tonnage:—

		Tons.	Dollars.
Steamers	60	21,500	1,500,000
Propellers	20	6,000	350,000
Brigs	50	11,000 }	
		}	2,000,000
Schooners	270	42,000 }	
	— —	— — —	— — — — —
Total	400	80,500 *	3,850,000 *

* - totals corrected

"In this we enumerate the seven Oswego propellers, and such sail craft belonging to Lake Ontario only as we know participate in the business of the upper lakes.

"On the stocks.—The desire to invest farther capital in vessels is seen in the number of new craft now on the stocks at various places throughout the whole range of the lakes. At this early day, we hear of the following to be rapidly pushed towards completion:

"At this port, a steamer of 750 tons, for Mr. Reed, the iron steamer Dallas, of 370 tons, for government, and three propellers of large size; at Chippewa, C. W., a large steamer; at Euclid, O., a brig of 290 tons; at Conneaut, O., a brig of 300 tons; at Cleveland, O., a steamer of 700 tons, three propellers of 350 tons each, a brig of 280 tons, a schooner of 230 tons, and another of 70 tons, all to be out early; at Charleston, O., a steamer of 800 tons, a propeller of 350 tons, and a schooner of 200 tons. An Oswego house has an interest in the propeller: at Maumee City, O., two propellers of 350 tons each; at Truago, Michigan, a large steamer of 225 feet keel, for Captain Whitaker; at Detroit, a large steamer for Mr. Newbury, another for Captain Gager, and a third, of the largest class, for Captain Randall; at Palmer, Michigan, a propeller for Captain Easterbrooks; at Newport, Michigan, a steamer for the Messrs. Wards, and the frame of another but smaller boat, for the same firm, to run between Detroit and Port Huron.

"At Goderich, C. W., or vicinity, a propeller; at Milwaukie, a barque and brig, of large tonnage, 300 each. One of these vessels is nearly planked up already, and will be down with a cargo of wheat as soon as the straits are navigable; at Depere, W. T., a large-sized schooner, and a yacht of 70 tons; at Chicago, a large brig, or schooner, for Captain Parker, late of the Indiana; at St. Catherine's, C. W., a brig; and at the mouth of the Genesee River a propeller, for a Rochester company, making, in all, ten steamers, twelve propellers, and twelve sail vessels—thirty-four in all."

Another American paper, in its remarks on the preceding article, furnishes some additional information.

"The introduction of steam upon the lakes was gradual, yet commensurate with our wants. From the building of the second boat, in 1822, to the launch of the Sheldon Thompson, at Huron, in 1830, six or seven small steamers had only been put in commission, and for the ensuing four years a press of business kept in advance of the facilities. But the zeal and extended desire to invest capital in new steamers was reached in 1837-8, when no less than thirty-three boats, with an aggregate of 11,000 tons, were built at an outlay of 1,000,000 dollars. This period points to the maximum, and then came the reaction. In 1840, only one steamer came off the stocks, and the same prostration and dearth in this department continued for three years, when it again received a new and fresh impulse, and now presents one of the leading characteristics of investment in our inland trade. The sum of 1,000,000 dollars has been diverted from other channels of business to this branch within the past two years, in addition to a very large outlay in sail vessels; and as the wants of commerce develop, some marked changes may be observed. The small, or medium-sized boats, into which the merchant farmer and foreign immigrant were indiscriminately huddled, have given place to capacious, swift, and stately vessels, in which are to be found a concentration of all that is desirable in water conveyance. Such is now the characteristic of steamboat building on the western lake.

"The following is the number and value of vessels owned and exclusively engaged in the trade of Upper Canada in 1844:—

	Dollars.
51 Steamers valued at	1,220,000
5 Propellers	46,000
80 Sail Vessels	114,000
	— — — —
Total, 136 Vessels	1,380,000
Having employed thereon 3,000 men.	

"The whole number of men employed between Buffalo and Chicago is estimated at about 5,000. During the season of non-navigation, half of these are employed upon farms in Ohio.

"Demonstrable evidence from many sources is at command to show the progressive change and accumulative power of the lake trade. In 1827, a steamer first visited Green Bay, for government purposes, and the Black Hawk war in 1832 drew two boats to Chicago for the first time. Now the trade of the latter place, in connexion with the business growing out of the rapid settlement of Wisconsin, sustains a daily line. A glance at the trade of Chicago for last year will illustrate the change that has taken place there.

"The gross tonnage of the lakes above the Falls, in 1845, was 100 vessels and 80,000 tons. This spring it will be found to have augmented from 5,000 to 10,000 tons.

"In 1845, the whole number of arrivals at the port of Buffalo was 1,700. Last season, 1,320 entries were made at Chicago. The entries at the port of Buffalo for 1845 were—

		Tons		Arriv.	Ag. ton.
Steamers	42	18,000		1,000	385,167
Propellers	9	2,550		76	23,477
Brigs	46	10,000	}		
			}	1,625	50,818
Schooners	211	40,000	}		
	— —	— — —			— — — —
Total	308	70,550			*459,462

*-total corrected

"From a valuable table given by the "Commercial Advertiser," we learn that the available steam marine of the lakes is 60 steamers, and a tonnage of 30,000 tons. This is irrespective of 20 propellers."

If the spirit of trade locates any where on this earth of ours, it does so specially at Buffalo, where dollars and cents, cents and dollars, occupy almost every thought of almost every mind. It is very amusing to look at the advertisements in a Buffalo paper. I shall give two or three as specimens.

Another Lot of those worsted dress goods, at one dollar a pattern, received this morning.

A. Wattles.

French Corded Skirts. Another lot of those French corded skirts just received, and for sale at

J. G. Latimer's, 216, Main Street.

Crash, Crash. Pure linen crash, slightly damaged, at half price at

Wattles' Cheap Store.

What kind of goods do you want? Ladies and gentlemen can find every kind of goods they may wish, in the dry goods line, at Garbutt's, plain or fanciful, any kind of dress you are in want of. Call at the Big Window, 204, Main Street.

Running off again. After Friday next, I shall commence running off my beautiful stock of Paris muslins and Balzorines, at great reduction.

N. B. Palmer, 194, Main Street.

History of Oregon, by George Wilkes, 25 cents.

T. S. Hawkes.

Gaiter Pants made to order, No. 11, Pearl Street.

E. W. Smith.

Voice of the People. Need not force them down. Sugar-coated Indian vegetable pills.

G. B. Smith.

Illustrations of the most ridiculous kinds show that newspaper advertisements must be very cheap indeed, for everything literally, from a washing-tub to a steamboat, is advertised daily for sale at Buffalo.

Buffalo is a sample city of the lake frontier of the United States, better than Rochester, a more manufacturing mill-power place; a specimen of what enterprise, energy, and paper money credit can do: a specimen of the border population, where hatred to England reigns supreme among the lower classes, and where a residence of six months would quite cure any English ultra-radical destructive of good education; an ultra-radical destructive of no education, or half educated, would, however, be vastly improved.

I had a soldier with me, and he asked leave to go on shore, which I freely granted, convinced, from what I knew of him, that he was proof against Buffalonian eloquence. He had scarcely stepped out of the vessel, on the wharf, in plain clothes, before he was hailed by a deserter, who was doing duty as a porter to some shopkeeper, and told of the delights of liberty and independence; but the porter had left the regiment for a little false estimate of the words meum and tuum, and therefore the old soldier declined turning from the carrying of Brown Bess [3] to being a beast of burden. He was then assailed by a sergeant, who had been obliged to desert for misconduct in a pecuniary point of view, and shown into a little grog-shop on the quay, that he was keeping; but appearances were here not very flattering either: in short, the deserter is not at a premium in the United States, for he is always suspected. Strange to say, these men are occasionally enlisted in the regular American army; a proof of which was witnessed last winter at Sackett's Harbour, where some of our officers from Kingston saw a man who had been received, and who had deceived all the American officers, except the surgeon. This gentleman, suspecting he was not a free and enlightened citizen, although he assumed the drawl and guess, suddenly said to him, "Attention!" upon which the deserter immediately dropped his hands straight, and stood, confessed, a soldier.

It would appear that in peace-time deserters should not be received into the ranks of a friendly power. Even in war, they are received by European nations with difficulty and distrust; for a man who once voluntarily breaks his oath and casts off his allegiance is very likely to be a double traitor.

The deserters from the regiments stationed in Canada frequently apply to be received back, but it is a rule to refuse them; and very properly so.

It is incredible what pains are taken on the frontier, by the loafing population from the States, to persuade the young soldiers to desert; and that, too, without any adequate prospect of benefit, but merely out of hatred, intense hatred, to England; for they soon leave the unfortunate men, who usually are plied with liquor, to their fate, when once in the land of liberty; and this fate is almost invariably a very miserable one.

The soldier I had with me told me that, while we were at the Falls, a man made up to him at the hotel, for he was then in uniform, being on the British side, and introduced himself as a general, saying that he was surprised he could remain in such a service, and volunteered to place him in their army, which he laughed at, and told him he preferred Queen Victoria's. This man he described to me as a gentleman, in his dress and manner; but, if he was a general, he was certainly a militia one, for the regular generals are not very plenty; and, from what I have heard of them, are above such meanness.

We had a military general, who is, I believe, a shoemaker of Buffalo or of New York, at Kingston last winter, who gave out that he had crossed over the ice to see if it was true that fortifications were actually in progress at Kingston. He met a keen young gentleman, who was determined to have a little fun with General Crispianus, who was attired in a fine furred, frogged, winter coat, and pointed Astracan cap, with a heavy tassel of silk.

"So you are at work here, I guess?"

"Yes," said the young gentleman, "we are."

"Well, I do hope you will be prepared in Kanaday, for though we don't approve some of our president's notions, we shall sustain him to a man; and, as soon as ever war is declared, we shall pour two or three hundred thousand men into your country and annex it."

"Oh, is that all!" replied the youth; "I advise you then, general, to take care of yourself, for we expect sixty thousand regulars from England."

"I didn't hear that before," said General Crispianus; and no doubt he returned to his last somewhat discomfited. Ne sutor ultra crepidam.

Before his departure, however, he went to see a newly invented pile-driver, which was at work, and, after looking at the monkey for some time, which was raised and lowered by two horses, and drove the piles very quickly, with enormous power, he said to his friend suddenly, "Waal, I swar, that does act sassy."

So much for General Crispianus.

We passed the night aboard of the Thames, preferring her spacious accommodations to those of the hotels in such a hot season, when the rain poured in torrents; but sleep was out of the question, for the climate of Sierra Leone could scarcely be more insufferable than the atmosphere then and there.

The rain cleared away in the morning, and a prospect of Lake Erie in a rage presented itself; so we could not quit the miserable apology for a harbour which Buffalo Creek affords, crowded, narrow, and nasty, until half past nine, and then, with great difficulty, on board the Emerald, a small Canadian steamboat, worked out amidst a string or maze of all sorts of merchant-craft.

Lake Erie presented an appearance exactly like the shallow sea, green and foamy, and very angry; and, in passing the shoals at the entrance of the Niagara river, it rolled the boat so that there was some danger; and one old lady vowed that she would never quit the United States any more.

A nice comfortable-looking Massachusetts farmer, the very type of a Buckinghamshire grazier of the year 1800, who was her husband, took a fancy to me because I was endeavouring to assure his old dame that she was not in real danger, and told me various stories, for he was very loquacious.

Among other things, he said it was very disgraceful to the Buffalonians to allow such a miscreant as Benjamin Lett, whom we saw on the wharf, be at large, as he boasted of having blown up Brock's monument, and of shooting Captain Ussher in cool blood at his own door in the night, long after all the disturbances of the insurrection were over. Lett seemed to glory in his villanies, and was a disgusting-looking loafer, for whose punishment the laws of the United States have proved either too lenient or totally inadequate. This fellow escaped when heavily ironed by jumping out of a rail car on his way to the Auburn Penitentiary, and no doubt has many admirers.

The good farmer told me that he had been to see Auburn, and that there was a little boy confined there for setting fire to a barn. He was only eleven years of age, and had been hired for half a dollar by a ruffian to do the deed.

But Auburn (what a misnomer for a penitentiary establishment, enough to make poor Goldsmith shiver in his shroud!) is not the only penitentiary in America where children expiate crime. Kingston in Canada can show several examples, among others, three brothers; and it appears to me that a better system is required in both countries. A house of correction for such juvenile offenders would surely be better than to mix them in labour with the hardened villains of a penitentiary. It is, in fact, punishing thought before it has time to discriminate, and the consequence is that these children return youths to the same place, and when they again leave it as youths, they return as men, for their minds are then callous.

The penitentiary system in Canada is undergoing a strict trial.

It will surprise my readers to state that, in an agricultural country, where the manners of the people are still very primitive, where education is still backward, and civilization slowly advancing, out of a population of about 1,200,000, scattered widely in the woods, there should be so large a proportion as twenty women, and five hundred men, in the Kingston Penitentiary; for, as education and civilization advance, and large towns grow up, new wants arise, and evil communication corrupts good manners, so that the proportion of great crimes between an old and a new country is much in favour always of the latter.

Recent discoveries of the police in Montreal have shown that hells of the most atrocious character, and one in imitation of Crockford's, as far as its inferior means would go, have been found out.

At Kingston a most wretched establishment of the same nature has recently been broken up, and at Toronto great incentives to vice in the very young exist.

Clerks in banks have gambled away the property of their employers in these places to the amount of several thousands, and, the frontier of the United States being so near, they have fled as soon as discovery was apprehended, but, owing to the international arrangements for the arrest of such criminals, have hitherto been detected, and consigned to the laws of their offended country.

The spirit of insubordination, which so forcibly operates in uneducated minds, where the constant example of the excess of freedom in the neighbouring States is ever present, has much changed the aspect of society in all the large towns and villages of Western Canada. There is no longer that honest independence of the working and labouring classes which existed fifteen years ago, but impudent assumption has forced its way very generally, and among servants more particularly. If they are not permitted to make the kitchen a rendezvous for their friends, to go out whenever they like, and in fact to be masters and mistresses of the habitation, they immediately, and without warning, leave, and no laws exist to prevent the growing evil: the consequence is that household economy is every where deranged, and a place, as it is called, is only good where high life below stairs is freely permitted.

The servants too are chiefly Irish, who have neither means nor inclination for settling in the forest, and consequently there is little or no competition, while they are so well known to each other, and so banded in a sort of Carbonari system, that it is extremely difficult to replace bad ones, even by worse.

The women servants are the worst. I saw an instance lately however of a precocious young villain of twelve, who was footboy in a gentleman's family, and his young sister, not fourteen, under-housemaid. His mother, a widow in infirm health, recently imported from Dublin, had brought up her children well, as far as reading and writing went, but had indulged them too much, and beat them so much, that they neither loved nor feared her. The little boy, only twelve, got into bad company, and ran away from his place, where he was well fed, well clothed, and kindly treated, and took his livery with him. He was brought back, after being partially frost-bitten, by his uncle, and received again from mistaken kindness. A cook of bad habits and worse temper got hold of him, and, after staying a short time, he again deserted with all the clothes and things he could carry. A young lady in the family had previously told him that her father would one day take him to the penitentiary to show him what bad boys came to. "That is the very place I want to get into," said the young ruffian, "for I hear there is fine fun there; I will steal something by and by, and then they will send me there."

Accordingly, he did steal, and took French leave one fine morning with Madam Cookey, having previously strangled the young lady's favourite cat, just about to kitten, and having the night before he absconded told the young lady he had made a famous nest for pussy to kitten in, and that if she went to the cellar in the morning, she would find the cat on her nest.

The young lady thought nothing of what he said at the moment, but, after finding when the family got up that the cook and boy were off, she went to look at her kittens, found the cat strangled, frozen, and placed on the nest. A day or two afterwards, the little sister decamped with three suits of dresses. Now what use would there be in putting such a boy or such a girl at so tender an age, and with such principles, into a penitentiary?

Penitentiaries are not proper receptacles for infant villains. The very contagion of working with murderers, coiners, horse-stealers, and scoundrels of the deepest dye is enough alone to confirm their habits and inclinations; and I am not aware of any instance of an infant boy or girl coming out of the Kingston Penitentiary subdued or improved. They are more marked characters when they again join their former friends; for they seldom avoid their former haunts and those whose example first led them astray, but plunge again and again deeper into crime.

It is the same with beating a child to excess; spare the rod and spoil the child, says the Jewish lawgiver; but where slavery does not exist, the rod is not to be used to that extent, and it does not improve even slaves. No; as in the army and in the navy, it hardens culprits, and very seldom indeed acts upon their consciences.

Border population is usually of a low character, and I cannot think it can be worse anywhere than where the maritime, or rather laculine, if such a word is admissible, preponderates, and where that race are unemployed for at least five months of the Boreal winters of Canada. It is only a wonder that serious crime is so infrequent. Burglary was almost unknown, as well as highway robbery, until last year; but instances of both occurred near Toronto, and the former twice at Kingston. The only use to such a class that a war could be of would be to employ them; but it is to be predicted, if peace exists much longer, that the civil and criminal jurisprudence of towns and cities bordering on the great lakes must undergo very great revision, and a suitable police be employed in them.

Nothing can, by any possibility, be more eminently absurd than the police of Kingston as at present constituted. These men are dressed like officers in the army; and, instead of being in the streets to prevent accident or crime, are employed, as they say, hard at work, detecting the latter. How they do now and then, at intervals few and far between, succeed in detecting an unhappy loafer is a mystery to everybody, for they are usually observed on the steps of the Town Hall, or carrying home provisions from the market, with a fine dog following them, or else jaunting about in cabs or sleighs.

London is said to have suffered much by the policemen finding their way down the area steps of houses, and amusing themselves in cupboard courtships with the lady-cooks, housemaids, and scullions; but I verily believe Kingston has not arrived at that perfection of a domestic police, for most of the men are middle-aged and married.

The cabmen and carters of Kingston, it is said, elect the Aldermen and Common Council. Whether this be true or false, I cannot pretend to say, but it is very certain that a more insolent, ungoverned race than the cabmen do not exist anywhere. The best position of the best promenade is occupied by these fellows; and no respectable female or timid man dares to pass them without receiving coarse insult; and, if complaint is made, they mark the complainant; and, if they keep a sleigh or carriage, make a point of running races near them, and cracking heavy whips to frighten their horses. One of these ruffians frightened a gentleman's horse last winter, and threw him, his wife, and daughter on the pavement, in consequence of the animal running away, and overturning the vehicle they were in. They know all the grooms and servants, and act according as they like or dislike them, caring very little what their masters hear or see. The carters are somewhat better, as there are decent men among them; but many of that body care very little about the laws of the road, which, by the by, are different here from those at home.

> If you go left you go right,
> If you go right, you go wrong,

is reversed in Canada, the right side of the road being always the driving side in both provinces; thus, if you go right, you do not go wrong; although such a manifest advantage in ethics, it will appear that right is not always right in Canada, but that cabmen's right and carters' right confer degrees in the Corporation College, which ensure a large share of wrong to the public.

But they are going to change all this, and bring in an Act of Parliament to alter the constitution of the fathers of the city of Regiopolis, who, it appears, have not hitherto rendered any account of their stewardship.

I shall not now enter into any further recapitulation of the journey from the Falls of Niagara to Toronto, or from Toronto to Kingston, save to say that some very intelligent citizens of the United States from Philadelphia were my companions on board the splendid British mail-packet, City of Toronto. The ex-Mayor of Philadelphia and his two amiable daughters were of the party, and I much question whether we could have had a more pleasant voyage than that which terminated on the seventeenth day of July. I omitted to observe, that voyage from Buffalo to Toronto was performed in eight hours and a quarter, as follows: Buffalo to Chippewa, by Emerald steamer, one hour and a half; Chippewa, by horse-car railway, to Queenston, one hour and a quarter; Queenston, by Transit steamer, to Toronto, four hours and a half, including all stoppages and detentions, among which was that of upwards of an hour at Queenston, waiting for the boat. The distance is about seventy miles; and the actual rate of going, for none of the conveyances are very rapid ones, is about ten miles an hour.

Kingston is one hundred and eighty-nine miles from Toronto by land, and one hundred and eighty by water; and the journey is performed in the mail-packets, which stop at several places occasionally, in eighteen hours, or about ten miles an hour, with detention for taking in wood, the speed averaging eleven.

CHAPTER XVII.

Equipage for a Canadian Gentleman Farmer—Superiority of certain iron tools made in the United States to English—Prices of Farming Implements and Stock—Prices of Produce—Local and Municipal Administration—Courts of Law—Excursion to the River Trent—Bay of Quinte—Prince Edward's Island—Belleville—Political Parsons—A Democratic Bible needed—Arrogance of American politicians—Trent Port—Brighton—Murray Canal in embryo—Trent River—Percy and Percy Landing—Forest Road—A Neck-or-nothing Leap—Another perilous leap, and advice about leaping—Life in the Bush exemplified in the History of a Settler—Seymour West—Prices of Land near the Trent—System of Barter—Crow Bay—Wild Rice—Healy's Falls—Forsaken Dwellings.

"A truant disposition" took me into another district on my return to Kingston, as I was thoroughly determined to see a thoroughly new Canadian settlement, and therefore prepared, by purchasing a new waggon and a new pair of horses, to start for Seymour West, in the Newcastle district, some 120 miles north-west, and upwards of twenty miles in the Bush from the main stream of settlement, where a young friend was beginning life, for whom the horses, waggon, and sundry conveniences for farming and a few little luxuries were intended.

A waggon, dear settling reader, in Canada, is not a great lumbering wooden edifice upon four wheels, whose broad circumferences occupy about four feet of the road, and contain some ton or two of iron, as our dear Kentish hop-waggons are wont to show in the Borough of Southwark, or throughout lordly London, those carrying coals. No, it is a long box, painted green or red, a perfect parallelogram, with two seats in it, composed of single boards, and occasionally the luxury of an open-work back to lean against; which boards are fastened to an ash frame on each side, thus affording an apology for a spring seat. This is the body; the soul, or carriage, by which said body is moved, consists of four narrow wheels, the fore pair traversing by a primitive pin under the body, the hind pair attached to the vehicle itself. A pole, or, as it is called, a tongue, projects from the front, and can be easily detached; et voilà tout! The expense is sixteen pounds currency, or about twelve sterling for a first-rate article, with swingle bars, or, as they are always called here, "whipple-trees," to attach the traces to. A set of double harness is six pounds, and two very good horses may be obtained for thirty more, making in all fifty-two pounds Canada money, or a little more than forty sterling, for an equipage fit for a gentleman farmer's all work, namely, to carry a field, or to ride to church and market in.

There are two or three other things requisite, and among the foremost a first-rate axe. No man should ever travel in Canada without an axe, for you never know, even on the great main roads, when you may want it to remove a fallen tree, or to mend your waggon with. A first-rate axe will cost you, handle and all, seven shillings and sixpence currency, but then it is a treasure afterwards; whereas, a cheap article will soon wear out or break. Strange to say, Sheffield and Birmingham do not produce coarse cutting tools for the Canada market, that can compete with the American. It has been remarked, of late years, that even all carpenters' tools, and spades, pickaxes, shovels, et id genus omne, are all cheaper, better, and more durable from the States, than those imported from England. Let our manufacturers at home look to this in time, and, eschewing the spirit of gain, cease to make cutting tools like Peter Pindar's razors. In the finer departments, such as surgical and other scientific instruments, Jonathan is as far astern; and, although he may use a sword-blade very well, he has not yet made one like Prosser's.

In heavy ironwork Jonathan is advancing with rapid strides; and even the Canadian, whom he looks down upon with some contempt, is competing with him in the forging and casting of steam-engines. There are very respectable foundries at Kingston, Toronto, Niagara, and Montreal. The only difficulty I have yet heard of is in making large shafts. Every other kind of heavy iron or steel manufacture can now be rapidly and better done in Canada than in the United States—I say advisedly better done, because the boilers made in Canada do not burst, nor do the engines break, as they do in the charming mud valley of the Mississippi. For one accident in Canada there are five hundred in the States; in fact, I remember only one by which lives were lost, and that happened to a small steamer near Montreal, about four years ago; whereas, they go to smash in the Union with the same go-ahead velocity as they go to caucus, and seem to care as little about the matter. John Bull often calculates much more sedately and to the purpose than his restless offspring, who seem to hold it as a first principle of the declaration of independence that a man has a right to be blown up or scalded to death.

They are as national in this as in naming new cities. What names, by the by, they do give them!—think of Alphadelphia in Michigan, Bucyrus in Ohio, Cass-opolis, from, I suppose, General Cass, in Michigan, Juliet in Illinois, Kalida (it ought to be Rowland Kalydor) in Ohio, Milan in Ohio, Massilon in Ohio, Peru in Iowa, Racine in Wisconsin, Tiffin in Ohio, and Ypsilanti in Michigan. Cæsar, Pompey, Cassius, Brutus, Homer, Virgil, and all the heathen gods, goddesses, demi-gods, and republicans, are sown as thick as leaves in Vallombrosa.

But to return to farming. You may have a plough, of the hundred new Yankee inventions, or of a good substantial Canadian cut, for six dollars, a wheat cradle scythe for the same, complete, a common scythe for ten shillings, or less; and thus for less than one hundred pounds, the farm may be stocked with two horses, two bullocks, two cows, (a good cow is worth five pounds) pigs, and poultry. Sheep you must not attempt, until a sufficient clearance of grazing ground is completed, but you can buy as many there as you want, of the very best kind, for three or four dollars a head. A good ram, bull, or boar, is, however, scarce, and proportionably dear, but most of the districts now have agricultural societies, at whose meetings prizes are given for every kind of stock, and the farmers are devoting much more of their attention to rearing horses, cattle, sheep, and pigs, than was the case ten years ago, when almost all the markets were supplied from the United States. Kingston and Toronto now are supplied from their own bulk; and, as it will interest an emigrant intending to settle, I shall give the market prices of both cities, premising only that, in country towns, provision of all kinds is much cheaper.

Toronto, January 2, 1846.

	s.	d.		s.	d.
Flour, per barrel, 196 lb	25	0	@	28	0
Oatmeal, per barrel, 196 lb	17	6	...	20	0
Wheat, per bushel, 60 lb	4	9	...	5	3
Rye, per bushel, 56 lb	2	9	...	3	0
Barley, per bushel, 48 lb	2	4	...	2	9
Oats, per bushel, 34 lb	1	10	...	2	2
Peas, per bushel, 60 lb	2	6	...	3	0

	s.	d.		s.	d.
Timothy, per bushel, 60 lb	4	0	...	5	0
Beef, farmers', per 100 lb	12	6	...	17	6
Beef, per lb	0	3	...	0	4
Pork, farmers', per 100 lb	21	3	...	27	6
Bacon, per lb	0	4	...	0	6
Mutton, by the quarter, per lb	0	2	...	0	3
Veal, by the quarter, per lb	0	2	...	0	4
Butter, in roll, per lb	0	8	...	0	10
Butter, in tub, per lb	0	7	...	0	9
Turkeys, each	1	3	...	3	9
Geese, each	1	3	...	1	6
Ducks, per couple	0	10	...	1	3
Chickens, per pair	0	10	...	1	3
Eggs, per dozen	1	3	...	1	3
Potatoes, per bushel	3	0	...	2	3
Hay, per ton	70	0	...	90	0
Straw, per ton	40	0	...	50	0

Kingston, January 31, 1846.

	s.	d.		s.	d.
Flour, per 112 lb	14	0	@	14	6
Oatmeal, per 112 lb	14	6	...	0	0
Wheat, per bushel	5	0	...	5	6
Barley, ditto	3	0	...	3	3
Hay, per ton	47	6	...	52	6
Straw, ditto	25	0	...	30	0
Potatoes, per bushel	2	0	...	2	3
Beef, per hundred	20	0	...	22	6
Veal, per lb	0	3	...	0	4
Mutton, ditto	0	3	...	0	4
Butter, in roll	0	9	...	0	10
Eggs, per dozen	0	9	...	0	10
Turkeys, per couple	5	0	...	7	6
Partridges, per pair	5	0	...	0	0
Ducks, per couple	1	8	...	2	0

The standard weights of grain and pulse, in Canada West, were regulated by Act of Parliament in 1835.

	lbs.
Wheat	60
Rye	56
Peas	60
Barley	48
Oats	34
Beans	50
Indian Corn	56

Equal to a Winchester bushel.

The price of keeping one horse in Kingston is about sixpence per day, in Toronto a shilling, but much less in all country places.

The affairs of the districts into which Canada is divided are managed by a warden and councillors in each district, and two councillors are elected for each township, having above 300 qualified voters, and one for each having a less number. The improvement of the district roads, bridges, schools, jails, court-houses, and all public matters requiring expenditure of the taxes raised within the district, are arranged by this Board. Some very useful information for settlers is contained in the following:—

Statute Labour.—Every male inhabitant, from twenty-one to sixty, not rated on the Assessment Roll, is liable to work on the highways for two days.

Every assessed inhabitant is, in proportion to the estimate of his real and personal property on the Roll, liable to work on the highways, as follows:— Under £25 two days; under £50 three days; from that to £75 four days; from that to £100 five days; and

For every	£50	above	£100,	up to	£500,	one day;
"	100	"	500,	"	1000,	"
"	200	"	1000,	"	2000,	"

"	300	"	2000,	"	3500,	"
"	500	"	3500,	one day.		

the fractional part between the different sums being always reckoned as a whole, and giving one day.

Every person possessed of a waggon, cart, or team of horses, [4] oxen, or beasts of burthen or draft, used to draw the same, is liable to work three days.

Indigent persons, oppressed by sickness, age, or having a large family, can be exempted at the discretion of the town warden.

Any person liable can commute at 2s. 6d. per day, if he thinks proper.

THE GENERAL ASSESSMENT.

By the 59th Geo. III., chap. 7, sect. 2nd, the following is deemed rateable property at the given valuation:—

Every town-lot in Toronto, Kingston, Niagara, and Queenston, £50; every town-lot in Cornwall, Sandwich, Johnstown, and Belleville, £25; every town-lot on which a dwelling is erected in Brockville, £30; do. in Bath, £20; every acre of arable, pasture, or meadow land, 20s.; every acre of uncultivated land, 4s.; every house built with timber, squared or hewed on two sides, of one story in height, and not two stories, with not more than two fireplaces, £20; for every additional fireplace, £4; every dwelling-house built of squared or flatted timber on two sides, of two stories in height, with not more than two fireplaces, £30, and for every additional fireplace, £8; every framed house under two stories in height, with not more than two fireplaces, £35, and for every additional fireplace £5; every brick or stone house of one story in height, and not more than two fireplaces, £40; every additional fireplace, £10; every framed, brick, or stone house, of two stories in height, and not more than two fireplaces, £60; every additional fireplace, £10; every grist-mill wrought by water, with one pair of stones, £150; every additional pair, £50; every sawmill, £100; every merchant's shop, £200; every storehouse owned or occupied for the receiving and forwarding of goods, wares, or merchandize, for hire or gain, £200; every stud-horse, kept for hire or gain, £100; every horse of the age of three years and upwards, £8; oxen of the age of four years and upwards, per head, £4; milch cows, per head, £3; horned cattle, from the age of two years to four years, per head, £1; every close carriage with four wheels, kept for pleasure, £100; every phaeton, or other open carriage, with four wheels, kept for pleasure only, £25; every curricle, gig, or other carriage, with two wheels, kept for pleasure only, £20;

every waggon kept for pleasure only £15; every stove in a room where there is no fireplace to be considered a fireplace.

All lands are rateable, held in fee-simple, or promise of fee-simple, by the land board certificate, order of council, or certificate of any governor of Canada, or by lease. The sum levied in no case to be greater than one penny in the pound for any one year.

The Queen, should she be possessed of, or in occupation of any property in the province, is exempted from the payment of taxes.

Each township of a district elects its own officers; at meetings held annually, on the first Monday in January, and called by the township clerk, after he has obtained a warrant from two or more justices of the peace. All freeholders above twenty-one years of age are entitled to a vote, and choose the undermentioned officers, viz.—one assessor and a collector, with pound-keepers and path-masters, or overseers of highways, three town-wardens, and from three to eighteen fence-viewers, whose duty it is to regulate fences. These town-officers are liable to penalty for refusing to serve, but cannot be elected oftener than once in three years: they have cognizance of all matters relating to cattle, height and nature of enclosures, and nuisances. Their duties are regulated by the district council's by-laws.

Each district has an inspector of licenses, deputy clerk of the crown, judge and clerk of District Court, a judge and a registrar of the Surrogate Court, and one or two registrars for deeds, with coroners, according to the extent, at all the principal towns or villages.

In each district is also a sheriff, a clerk of the peace, a treasurer, and, in some of the district towns, a board of police, with president, clerk, treasurer, and street-surveyor.

The officers of the incorporated cities or towns are similar to those at home.

Justice is administered by the courts of Queen's Bench, Quarter-Sessions, District Courts, and the Town Court, with Division Courts.

The terms of the Court of Queen's Bench are four; and in Western Canada, at these times, the judges sit at Toronto to hear counsel on law questions.

Easter term commences on the first Monday in February, and ends on the Saturday of the following week.

Trinity term, second Monday in June, and ends Saturday of the following week.

Michaelmas term, first Monday in August, until Saturday of the following week.

Hilary, first Monday in November, until Saturday, as before.

The Quarter Sessions are held throughout the province on the 7th of January, 1st of April, 1st of July, and 18th of November.

The District Courts are held at the same time as the Quarter Sessions. This court has jurisdiction in all matters of contract from 40s. to £15; and, when the amount is liquidated or ascertained, either by the act of the parties, or the nature of the transaction, to £40. Thus a promissory note under £40 can be sued in this court before the district judge, who is usually a barrister: and an open or unsettled account under £15, but none above that amount; also, all matters of wrong, or, as the lawyers please to call it, tort, respecting personal chattels, when title to land is not brought in question, and the damages are under £15. The judge of the District Court, by a late Act, presides also at Quarter Session.

The ordinary costs of a suit before him are from £5 to £10; and in the Queen's Bench, before a real judge, from £10 to £30.

The Division Courts are a sort of non-descript Courts of Conscience for recovery of small debts under £10; and here the district judge has his hands full, for he comes into play as president again, and has to hold courts in six divisions of his district once in two months.

The Court of Chancery is the summum bonum; its costs are, of course, very great, and its decisions, though not quite so protracted as those of England, nor involving such stakes, plague many a poor suitor who comes to equity, when he can no longer get justice. I should most strongly advise him to ponder deeply, after wading through Division, District, and Queen's Bench, through judges without a wig and gown to judges in full paraphernalia, and barristers and attorneys without end, before he encounters a Master in Chancery. It may be such a lesson as he will never forget, for Canada is rather a litigious country—it is too near the States to be otherwise, and lawyers, as well as all other trades and professions, must live. Young settler, stick to your farm, get a clear title to your land, and never get into debt.

I left Kingston in autumn, as aforesaid, with the farm stock and implements, and embarked on board the Prince Edward steamboat, Captain Bouter, for the mouth of the river Trent, in the Bay of Quinte.

First you steam along the front of the famous city of Kingston, which now presents something of an imposing front, from the waters of the St. Lawrence, which here leave Lake Ontario and contract into two channels between which are Long Island and some others. The channel nearest to the United States is very narrow, or about a mile; that on the Canada side is very broad, being from three to five or six, with an islet or rock in the centre of the mouth or opening of Lake Ontario, called Snake Island, having one tree upon it, and visible from a great distance.

A few miles above Kingston, you enter the Bay of Quinte by passing between the main land and Amherst Isle, or the Isle of Tanti, owned by Lord Mountcashell, on which are now extensive and flourishing farms. At the east end of the Isle of Tanti are the Lower Gap and the Brothers, two rocky islets famous for black bass fishing and for a deep rolling sea, which makes a landsman very sick indeed in a gale of wind. After passing this Scylla, the bay, an arm rather of Lake Ontario, becomes very smooth and peaceable for several miles, until you leave the pleasant little village of Bath, where is one of the first churches erected by the English settlers in Western Canada, and the beginning of the granary of the Canadas.

After passing Bath, the Upper Gap Charybdis gives you another tremendous rolling in blowing weather, and the expanse of Lake Ontario is seen to the left, with the tortuous bay of Quinte again to the right; this arm of the lake being made for fifty or sixty miles more by the fertile district of Prince Edward, an island of great extent, and one of the oldest of the British settlements in Upper Canada, where Pomona and Ceres reign paramount; for all is fertility.

The Bay of Quinte, in fact, on both the main shore and on Prince Edward, is one unvaried scene of the labours of the husbandman; for the forest is rapidly disappearing there, and the luxuriance of the scenery in harvest can only be compared with the best parts of England. It is indeed a glad and a rich country.

The Lake of the Mountain and the Indian village of Tyandinaga are the lions of this route: the former, a singular crater full of the purest water, on the summit of a hill of some altitude, without any apparent source, but overflowing in a stream sufficient for mill purposes and very deep; the latter the seat of a portion of the Mohawks already mentioned.

The vessel calls at several small settlements, and stops for the night at Hallowell or Picton, for the village has both names. This is a most picturesque locality, in a nook of the bay, with undulating hills and sharp ravines, a handsome church and other public edifices, and a large and thriving population. But we must for the present keep on board the steamer, and, after sleeping there, go on to Belleville, leaving Fredericksburgh, Adolphus Town, and many others in the Midland, to coast the Victoria district, and enter the charming little retreats in this pleasant bay to be described more at leisure.

Belleville, the county town of the Victoria district, is situated on the shores of this bay, and, from an insignificant village in 1837, has risen in 1846 to the rank of a large and flourishing town, the main street of which surprised me not a little by its extent, the beauty of its buildings, and the display of its shops. I mounted the hill-side which overlooks it, and there saw three fine churches, the English, Roman Catholic, and Scotch places of worship, a large well built court-house and jail, and some pretty country-houses. I should think that Belleville has nearly four thousand inhabitants; and, as it is the outlet of a rich back country, and on the main road from Kingston to Toronto, it will increase most rapidly. The worst feature about Belleville in 1837 was that it was the focus of American saddle-bag preachers, teachers, and rebelliously disposed folks; but I am told that most of these uneasy loafers have left it, and that its character has improved wonderfully. What a nuisance are peddling, meddling, politicians of the lowest grade? Wherever they plant their feet, a moral pestilence follows. These fellows won't work, for the voluntary principle in preaching or teaching pays better, and does not cost so much trouble. It is surprising with what facility, in England, as well as in Canada, a saddle-bag doctor of divinity takes his degree, and becomes possessor of the secrets and director of the consciences and household of the small farmer. I once knew a family, a most respectable family of yeomen, of ancient descent and of excellent hearts, devoured by a locust of this kind in Buckinghamshire. In Canada they are devoured every day, and not unfrequently made disloyal into the bargain, although deriving their lands and support originally from the British government.

They travel to the most remote settlements, where no such opportunities as church or chapel of any kind exist for public worship; and, after gaining the good opinion of the simple settler by an exterior sanctity and a snuffling expression of it, they soon slide into the recommendation of the superior chances of salvation that offer themselves, by forgetting the Divine command of "Render unto Cæsar the things that are Cæsar's," and of the Apostolic doctrine of "Honour the King." I have always been surprised that a democratic Bible retains such highly improper translations of the original tongue, as prince, king, queen, and conceive that there should be a special Act of Congress to declare that henceforward the words of the English language should be abolished and the American tongue substituted, under pains and penalties, omitting the aforesaid and all other similar obnoxiosities from dictionary, grammar, and book. The Americans have just discovered that they have a prior claim to Oregon, and therefore must be an older nation than the British, the separation being a mere trifle, and the sway of England over the thirteen colonies and her ancient settlement of America a dream; ergo, the American language is the primitive tongue. A very excellent worthy gentleman of New York wrote to a friend in Kingston lately, stating that he was sorry that England was going to such an expense in fortifying that town, as it and all Canada would soon be American, and then the money thrown away would be missed. [5]

It is actually astonishing, and will scarcely be credited at home, that all except the most reflecting people in the United States have, within the last five years, become really and seriously impressed with the notion that the whole continent of the New World is a part of their birthright, and that it is about to pass under their dominion, as a matter of course, as well as that all the powers of the Old World cannot hinder this consummation one day, or even exist themselves much longer, as a political millennium is speedily coming on.

As an example of the self-sufficiency of this feeling, I quote a letter from a governor of a State, lately written to his constituents, perhaps on the strength of re-election, but really developing the national notion. In reply to a letter addressed to him by the whigs of Chautauque county, desiring his consent to stand as one of their candidates for the delegates to the Constitutional Convention, ex-Governor Seward wrote a reply of which the following is an extract:—

"I want no war—I want no enlargement of territory sooner than it would come if we were contented with a masterly inactivity. I abhor war, as I detest slavery. I would not give one human life for all the continent that remains to be annexed.

"But I cannot exclude the conviction that the popular passion for territorial aggrandizement is irresistible. Prudence, justice, cowardice, may check it for a season, but it will gain strength by its subjugation. An American navy is hovering over Vera Cruz. An American army is at the heart of what was Mexico. Let the Oregon question be settled when it may, it will, nevertheless, come back again. Our population is destined to roll its resistless waves to the icy barriers of the north, and to encounter oriental civilization on the shores of the Pacific. The monarchs of Europe are to have no rest, while they have a colony remaining on this continent. France has already sold out. Spain has sold out. We shall see how long before England inclines to follow their example. It behooves us then to qualify ourselves for our mission. We must dare our destiny. We can do this, and can only do it by early measures which shall effect the abolition of slavery, without precipitancy, without oppression, without injustice to slaveholders, without civil war, with the consent of mankind, and the approbation of Heaven. The restoration of the right of suffrage to free men is the first act, and will draw after it in due time the sublime catastrophe of emancipation."

It is with nations as it is with individuals; a boy very soon fancies himself a man; he takes a switch in his hand, rides a muck against thistles and stinging nettles, cuts off their heads, might and main, and then fancies himself a Wellington or a Nelson. Young nations have the same notions, and age tames both the one and the other.

Texas was easily tampered with; it was peopled only to be the People's: but Mexico may be a harder bone to pick. Already is a newspaper published there, named El Tiemps, The Times, to advocate a return to monarchy, in order to save the Spanish race from the Stars and the Stripes; and the besotted and wretched Republics of the South, conceived in folly, and born of the splendid dream of Canning, are falling to pieces from internal wars. Will his Ophirian Majesty, the Emperor of Brazil, humbly lay his crown at the feet of the Eagle, and are all our West India islands to be sipped up in the spoon of the President?

Let the United States be a great, a free, and an enlightened Republic; no one in England desires otherwise. Let it hold the balance, to curb the semi-barbarous States of South America, and let it spread the gospel of peace, and the literature and laws of Britain to the uttermost parts of that benighted region; but also let it curb itself in time, before it seeks to overthrow all order, all rule, all right, and all reason, under the feet of its mere fancied might.

There is not in England that hatred of its American offspring, which exists so largely towards the Parent State in the Union; on the contrary, there is an earnest, a sincere desire for the well-being and advancement of its best interests; but it is useless to conceal, and it would be unmanly also to attempt to do so, that the British pulse does not beat in unison with Lynch law, or with mob-rule, any more than it would with the tyranny of a despotism; neither will the honest pride of the English, the Irish, or the Scotch, permit that mob dominion, the might of the mass, to dictate a line of conduct upon any question, territorial or gubernative. Many master-minds at home admire the principles of the American constitution, as established by Washington; but they deeply regret the gulf that has opened since the era of that law-giver; and there are few indeed who would dream even of exchanging the freedom of England for the freedom of the United States.

The Reformers of British origin in Canada are, no doubt, very numerous; and, owing to misconception and other causes, with which the public are now acquainted, were once desirous of hoisting a new flag; but time and reflection have been at work since, and the term reformer in Canada is no longer one with which a word of fewer syllables is synonymous. Even during the rebellion, as it was called, of 1837, but which more properly should be called the border troubles, there were very few Upper or Western Canadians concerned, as the brigands were chiefly American borderers; the real rebellion being confined to Lower Canada. I commanded a very large body of militia, much of which had been gathered from the districts and counties where the Reformers had their strongholds, and in the ranks there were full as many Reformers as there were Tories, as the other party were then called.

These subjects force themselves upon my attention, from the voyage near the shores of Sydney, Thurlow, and other townships, where Reformers and the really disaffected were very numerous in 1837; but, notwithstanding all this, it may be freely and fairly asserted again and again, that, let an invading force appear on their soil, the people of Canada will fight for home, for liberty, and for Queen Victoria.

We steamed on to the Trent river through a glorious corn and apple country, and arrived there in time to meet my young friend, and to proceed in our waggon to Brighton, a few miles westward on the Toronto road, where we slept.

Trent Port, or Trent village, is situated on both banks of the exitus of the Trent river into the Bay of Quinte, and is remarkable for two things: as being the intended outlet of one of the finest back countries in Canada, by a gigantic canal, which was to open Lake Huron to Ontario, through a succession of inland lakes and rivers, but which noble scheme was nipped in the bud after several of the locks had been excavated, and very many thousands of pounds expended. It is now remarkable only for its long, covered wooden bridge, and the quantity of lumber, i.e., in the new American Dictionary, deals, plank, staves, square timber, and logs floating on the tranquil water for exportation.

Brighton is a little pleasant high-road hamlet, with two inns, and no outs, as it is not a place of trade, excepting as far as a small sawmill is concerned; but this will change, for it is near Presqu'ile, the only natural harbour on Lake Ontario's Canada shore, from Toronto to Kingston, or from one end to the other. Here the Bay of Quinte approaches the lake so close, that a canal of four or five miles only is requisite, through a natural level, in order to have a safe and sheltered voyage from Kingston without going at all into the real and dangerous lake, which is every where beset with "ducks and drakes," as its rocky and treacherous islets are called.

This canal, which may be constructed easily for about five and twenty thousand pounds, must soon be made, and the bar of Presqu'ile Harbour deepened, so as to ensure a shelter for vessels in the furious gales of October and November.

The canal is always traced on maps, and called Murray Canal, I presume, after the late Master-General of the Ordnance, during his government of the province. It is, without doubt, one of the most important and necessary works in Canada West; and, as it will lead into the Trent navigation, when that shall be finished, will be the means of adding some millions of inhabitants to the fairest portion of the land, now known only to wretched lumbermen.

The River Trent is a large stream, full of shallows, and rapids, and beautiful lakes, taking its rise north of the township of Somerville, in the Colborne District, not very far from a chain of lakes, which reach the Ottawa on the east, and the Black River, a feeder of Lake Simcoe, and a tributary of Huron and the Severn, on the west.

The river Trent is strangely tortuous, but keeps almost entirely within the Colborne district, named after Lord Seaton, and at Rice Lake afforded a site for the Colonial Office to establish a flourishing colony a few years ago at Peterborough, and to open an entirely new and very rich portion of Canada West.

This river, placed, as it were, by Nature as the connecting link of a great chain of inland navigation, embracing the expanse of Huron, Ontario, and the Ottawa, opens a field of research both to the agriculturist and the forester. The woods abound with the finest kind of untouched timber; the land is fertile in the extreme; and the rivers, streams, and lakes abound with fish. In short, had the Trent Canal been finished, instead of the miserable and decaying timber-slides, which now encumber that noble river, another million of inhabitants would, in ten years more, have filled up the forests, which are now only penetrated by the Indian or the seeker after timber.

A private individual has, however, put a steamboat upon the centre of the river's course; and Mr. Weller, no doubt, finds that it pays him well, for the portion of Colborne district near Rice Lake is settling rapidly.

The Trent Canal, or a railroad, in the same direction, would lead to the Georgian Bay of Huron, and thus render a journey to the far West easy of accomplishment, as it is the most direct route from Oswego and New York.

But I must journey on, and, after resting at Brighton, start by daylight, and penetrate into the bowels of the land by a sandy road, which, after passing that village, stretches into the forest due north.

Away the waggon went, not at a hand-gallop, for the sand was too deep for that, and, passing through woods by a tolerably good road for so new a settlement, we, every now and then, at intervals few and far between, saw a new farm or a new log-hut.

The day was fine, and so, having carried our provision with us, we halted in the deep woods, upon the muddy banks of the Cold Creek, to breakfast. A Tartar camp was visited by an English traveller somewhere in the dominions of the Grand Lama, and he was treated to London porter. So were we in the deep forest of Central Canada, for London porter appears to travel everywhere; and, discussing it with much relish, we fed the horses, and gave them what they liked much better, clear and pure water—which indeed I now think would have been quite as good for us—and waggoned on, until we came to a surprising new settlement in the Bush, the villages of Percy and Percy Landing, where, there being mill "privileges," as a sharp running water-stream is called in the United States, flour and saw-mills have been established, and a very thriving population is rising both in numbers and in means. Here we dined in a new inn, or rather tavern, kept by a French Canadian, and then pursued our journey for a few miles on a decent new road, amidst fine settlements and good farms, and, crossing a beautiful stream, plunged into the undisturbed forest by a road in which every rut was a canal, and every stone as big as a bomb-shell at the very least. How the waggon stood it, and the roots and stumps of the trees with which these boulders were diversified, I am still unable to explain; for my part, I walked the greater part of it, for the bones of my body seemed as if they were very likely, after a short trial, to part company with each other.

At length, after jolting, jumping, complaining, and comforting, we came to a bridge near Myer's Mills. Our conducteur, my young friend aforesaid, who was more used to the road, saw at a glance that something had gone wrong with the said bridge; for it exhibited a very disorderly, drunken sort of devil-may-care aspect.

He was too far advanced upon it to retreat, when he discovered that a beam or two had departed into the lively current below. With true backwoodsman's energy, he pulled his horses up sharp, reined them well up, and then, with a tremendous shout, applied the whip, and actually leaped horses, waggon, and passengers over the chasm, the remainder of the bridge groaning, and saying most plainly, "I will not bear this any longer." Next morning, we heard that the whole structure had fallen in and disappeared.

I have been in some danger in the course of my life; but a visit afterwards to this spot convinced me that one's existence is often a sort of size-ace throw; and whether the six or the one comes up or goes down, is a miracle. I never had a nearer leap for clearing Styx than this, excepting one shortly afterwards upon the timber-slides of the Trent, at Healy's Falls.

A vast timber canal or way had been constructed here by the Board of Works, to convey timber down a rapid without danger, the slide being alongside of that rapid. It was an interesting work; and, with my young friend and two naval officers, settled in Seymour, I went to examine it. At the sluice-way, or timber-dam, was a sort of bridge, composed of parallel pieces of heavy square joists and a platform; we walked along this Mahomet's railway, where Azrael seemed to have established pretty much the same sentry as Cerberus, having two or three mouths ready to devour the adventurous passenger.

The parallel pieces were about two feet distant from each other; I walked on one, and my companions on the other, until a good view of the whole work and the splendid rapids was attained. Under our feet, at some distance, was the water of the slide running on an inclined plane of woodwork, at a great angle, and with enormous power and velocity into a pitch or cauldron far below.

The day was bright, and the shadow of the parallel logs left between the space no view of the water underneath. They called me suddenly to look at the rapid. I jumped, as I thought, over the space between us; but my jump was into the shadow. One of the naval officers, a powerful man, six feet and more in height, saw me jump; and, just as I was disappearing between the timbers, caught me by the arm, and, by sheer muscle and strength, held me in mid-air. The other immediately assisted him, but my young friend became deadly pale and sick. I did not visit either the slide or the cauldron; in either, instantaneous and suffocating death was inevitable. Reader, never leap in dark places, and look before you leap. My young friend looked before he leaped over the bridge with his span of horses, and, like a gallant auriga, guided his van without fear; but he told me afterwards that the cold sweat sat on his brow, when the chasm was cleared, as much on the bridge as it did at my Quintus Curtius venture. By the by, did Quinte Curce, as the French so adroitly call him, ever leap—I doubt the fact—into the chasm which closed over him?

After passing this bridge, and a slough of despond beyond it, we again plunged into the woods, and, mounting over boulders, sinking into bog-holes, and fairly jolted to jelly, on a sudden turned into an open space of near a hundred acres, round which the solemn and stately forest kept eternal guard. Here, in the space of ten or twelve years, our pioneer friends had laboured through weal and through woe, through Siberian winters and West Indian summers, through ague and fever, to create a little modern paradise,

My young friend commenced in this secluded region, where the outer barbarian was never seen and seldom heard of, where even the troubles of 1837-8 never showed themselves, his location upon one hundred acres. He had received the very best education which a public institution in England could afford; but circumstances obliged him, at the early age of twenty-five, to turn his thoughts, with a young wife, to "life in the Bush," as a sole provision. The partner of his cares, equally well educated, and of an ancient family, by the death of her father, who was high in office in his country's service, was left equally unprovided for.

With youth and good constitutions, a determination to make their own way in life spurred them on to the most disheartening task, a task which thousands of young people from Britain have, however, daily to encounter in Canada, and the progress of which I relate simply from a desire to show that "life in the Bush" is not to be entered into without solemn and serious reflection.

Their first undertaking was to clear an acre or two of the forest, and crop it with grain and potatoes; then to build a log-house. In all this they were assisted by friends and neighbours as far as the limited means of those friends and neighbours, who were all similarly engaged, and the settlement containing not more than four or five families, would admit of.

My young friend really set his shoulder to the wheel, and did not call upon Hercules whiningly. He had a fondness for carpenter's work, and, having cut down the huge pine trees on his lot, for so a property is called in Canada West, he hewed them, squared them, and dovetailed them; he quarried stone with infinite toil, burnt lime, and in the short space of two years had a decent log-palace, consisting of two large rooms, and a kitchen and cellar, with an excellent chimney, a well which he dug himself, and a very large framed barn, which he built himself, the only outlay being for nails, shingles to cover his roofs, and boards. These he had to bring with oxen and a waggon from the saw-mills at Percy, many miles off, and by the most hideous road I ever saw, even in Canada. He split his own rails, made his own fences, and cleared his own forest. This first settlement was commenced in 1840, and, when I saw it in 1845, he had nearly thirty acres cleared, and this clearance and his really good house let to a settler just arrived.

By one of those freaks of fortune unforeseen and unaccountable, a connexion, who occupied the adjacent farm of two hundred acres, and had had the command of money, died, and his property was left to the young couple.

This gentleman, in the course of six or seven years, from the first settlement of this portion of Canada, had built an excellent house, had cleared a hundred acres, had a good garden, and everything which a settler could desire, with a well-stocked farm-yard, and a well-furnished house, into which my young friend stepped from his log-palace and became monarch of all he surveyed.

But money, the sinews of war, was wanted; for, although the land, house, goods, and chattels became his, the funds went to another person, all but a trifling annual sum.

The young couple had now a family growing about them, and, as they were very old friends of mine, they asked me to come and see "life in the Bush."

Farmer Harry, as we will call my young friend, had now three instead of two hundred acres to attend to, but he had a flock of sheep, a pair of oxen, the span of horses I brought for him, several cows, much poultry, and a whole drove of pigs, with barns full of wheat, peas, hay, and oats; an excellent garden, a fine little brook full of trout at his door, plenty of meadow, and his harvest just over.

To help him, he had a hired man, who drove the oxen and assisted in ploughing; and to bring in his harvest there were three hired labourers, at two shillings and sixpence a day each, and their food and beds, with two maid-servants, one to assist in the dairy. Labour, constant and toilsome labour, was still necessary in order to make the farm pay; for there is no market near, and everything is to be bought by barter.

Salt, tea, sugar, and all the little luxuries must be had by giving wheat, peas, timber, oats, barley, the fleeces of the sheep, salted pork, or any other exchangeable property; and thus constant care and constant supervision of the employed, as well as constant personal labour, are requisite in Canada on a farm for very many years, before its owner can sit down and say, "I will now take mine ease."

The female part of the family must spin, weave, make homespun cloth, candles, salt the pork, make butter for sale, and even sell poultry and eggs whenever required; in short, they must, however delicately brought up, turn their hands to every thing, to keep the house warm.

The labour of bringing home logs for fuel in winter is not one of the least in a farm, and then these logs have to be sawed and split into convenient lengths for the fireplaces and stoves.

But all this may be achieved, if done cheerfully; and, to show that it can, I will add that, amidst all this labour, my young friend was building himself a dam, where the beavers, in times when that politic and hard-working little trowel-tailed race owned his property, had seen the value of collecting the waters of the brook. He was repairing their decayed labours, for the purpose of washing his sheep, of getting a good fish-pond, and of keeping a bath always full for the comfort of his family.

What a change in ten years! The forest, which had been silent and untrodden since the beavers first heard afar off the sound of the white men's axes, was now converted into a smiling region, in which a prattling brook ran meandering at the foot of gently swelling hill-sides, on which the snowy sheep were browsing, and the cattle lowing.

A field of Indian corn was rustling its broad and vivid green flaggy leaves, whilst its fruit, topped by long silky pennons, waving in the breeze, seemed to say to me, "Good Englishman, why do your countrymen despise my golden spikes? do they think, as they do of my ugly, prickly friend the oat, that I am not good enough for man, and fit only for the horse or the negro? You know better, and you have often eaten of a pound-cake made of my flour, which you said was sweeter and better than that of wheat. You have often tasted my puddings; come now, Mr. John Bull, were they not very good?"

"Certainly they were, Mr. Maize, and hominy and hoe-cake and all that sort of thing are good too; but pray don't ask me to devour you in the shape of mush, molasses and butter. Take any shape but that, and my firm nerves will never tremble."

Jesting apart, the flour of Indian corn, or maize, is as much superior, as nutritive food, to potatoes, as wheat flour is to Indian corn. I wish the poor Irish had plenty of it.

The farmers in Upper Canada use it much, but in that wheat country it cannot of course be expected that it supersedes flour, properly so called. They also use buckwheat flour largely in the shape of pancakes, and a most excellent thing it is.

My friend's life was diversified; for, during the season that the crops are ripening, he had time to spare to go out on fishing and shooting excursions on the Trent, and occasionally in winter a little deer-hunting, with, longo intervallo, a bear-killing event.

I went to a combined fishing and shooting pic-nickery, and travelled from Rainey's mills and Falls all along the valley of the Trent to Healy's Falls.

The Trent is a beautiful and most picturesque river, rushing and roaring along over a series of falls and rapids for miles together, and expanding in noble reaches and little lakes.

Rainey's Falls I have faintly sketched, to show the soft beauty of some parts of this river; at Healy's Falls it is more broken.

We went to Crow Bay, just above which the Crow River, from the iron mine country of Marmora, runs into the Trent. Here we found two friends, brothers, settled in great comfort. They had been about ten years in the "Bush," and had excellent farms and houses equal to any I have seen so far in the interior, with every comfort around them. In one of their pleasure-boats, we embarked for the junction of the rivers, on which it is intended to place a town when the country becomes more settled.

All is now forest, excepting a very extensive and very flourishing settlement of twelve hundred acres, undertaken by a retired field-officer in the army, which was a grant about ten years ago for his services, and is now worth two thousand pounds, or perhaps more, since a bridge has been built by the provincial legislature over the Trent, in order to connect the mail route between the townships of Seymour-East and Seymour-West, as both are filling up rapidly, and land becomes consequently dear and scarce.

The price of land in Seymour at present is, improved farm, if a good house and barns are on it, at least two pounds an acre, including clearance and forest; Canada Company's land, from fifteen to twenty shillings an acre; wild land, in lots of one hundred or two hundred acres; Clergy Reserve, or College land, called School land, according to situation, from twenty-five shillings an acre upwards to thirty, all wild land. Private Proprietors' wild land, in good situations, twenty shillings an acre, and very little for less. Along the river-banks, none, I believe, is to be had, unless at very high prices.

It is intended, no doubt, to complete the navigation of this splendid river by and by, and thus holders of land are not very anxious to sell at a cheap rate; and as the Board of Works has constructed, at an expenditure of upwards of twenty thousand pounds, timber slides, along all the worst rapids by which the lumber is taken to the mouth of the Trent, a certain importance is now attained for this river which did not before exist; but this is of very little use to Seymour, in which, new as the township is, all the best pine has already been culled and cut down by the lawless hordes of lumberers, who, of course, no longer consume any of the farm produce; yet it adds to the importance of the river generally.

The first settlers in Seymour were lumber merchants, who, seeing the wealth of the country in pine, and oak, and ash, the great fertility of the soil, and the facilities afforded everywhere for erecting mills, established themselves permanently, and, before the agriculturists were induced to think of it, had removed from all land within miles of the river the only valuable timber that the township contained. Thus one source of profit, and that a very great one to the farming settler, has been destroyed, and the enterprising timber-merchant has established at convenient distances several saw-mills, where his lumber is converted into plank and boards for the lower markets, and where he is at all times ready to saw whatever timber the farmer has left into boards and planks for him, receiving so many feet of timber, and giving so many feet of lumber, as sawed timber is called, taking care of himself, of course, in the exchange.

The flour-mills at Percy proceed upon the same principle: a farmer brings sacks of grain and receives sacks of flour in exchange, said exchange being of course three to one, or more, against him.

Throughout Canada is this truck or barter system pursued, and very little money finds its way either into or out of the back townships, unless it be the receipts of the lumber-merchant from Quebec or the lakes. The lumber-merchant is, therefore, the lord of the Trent, or of any other great internal river, whereon are new settlements; and many of them have amassed large fortunes.

Thus came timber-slides, instead of canal, upon this splendid river, which must, as soon as the Murray Canal, on the Bay of Quinte, is undertaken, be also opened to navigation, as by it the richest part of Western Canada, both in soil and in minerals, will be reached, and a direct communication had in war-time from Kingston, the great naval key of the lakes, with Penetangueshene, and Lakes Huron and Superior.

I have not time now, nor would it amuse the reader, to give a detail of the project for canalling the Trent, part of which was well executed before the troubles of 1837; but the money was voted, and is not so enormous as to justify the non-performance of so important a public work. The timber-slides I look upon as mere temporary expedients.

But let us launch upon Crow Bay, and, stealing silently along, get near the wild rice which grows so plentifully on its shallows, and where is found the favourite food of the wild duck, which, by the by, is no inconsiderable addition to a Canadian dinner-table in the Bush. I do not mean, reader, the wild duck, but the wild rice, which said duck eats; for, when well made into a rice pudding, I prefer it, and so do many who are greater epicures, to either Carolina or East India rice.

The wild ducks suffered not from me, for I had no gun, and, after crossing the rapid current of the junction of the rivers, we landed on the isthmus formed by them, where, striking a light, and making a fire, we bivouacked, and one of the party went in search of a deer, whose tracks were seen. This is a singular place, covered with dwarf oaks, on a sandy soil, and looking for all the world like an English park in Chancery.

Almost every oak bore the marks of bears' claws, as it was a favourite place for those hermits, who live on acorns, blackberries, wild gooseberries and currants, and I dare say raspberries, strawberries, and whortle-berries, with which the place abounds in their seasons. The boughs of the oaks were also broken by the repeated climbings of Bruin, and it must be somewhat dangerous, when he is very hungry, to land here and traverse the Bush alone: but we saw none, although we walked through it, admiring the rushing river, and occasionally going down the steep banks to fish in the rapids for black bass, of which several were caught, and, with several wild ducks, formed the day's sport, which day's sport was twice or thrice repeated, until I had seen as much of the beauty of the wild river and the nature of the soil and country as was desirable.

It was somewhat melancholy, on reaching Healy's Falls, which are turbulent rapids of the most picturesque character, with an immense timber-slide, or broad wooden sloping canal alongside of them, to see the clearance in this far solitude formed by the workmen. They had built houses, shanties, and sheds, and had lived and loved together for many a month, with their families, on this charming spot. Nothing was in ruin: all was new, even to the window-glass; and when our party, after toiling away through the forest, reached the opening, and saw below us the foaming rapids, the grand forest, the rugged banks, the timber-slide, and the little wooden town, we thought, here at least, is a well chosen hamlet, at which we may rest awhile.

No smoke rose from the chimneys; not a soul appeared to greet us; the eagle soared above; the cunning fox, or the murderous wolf, the snake and the toad, alone found shelter, where so many human beings had so recently congregated, where, from morn till dewy eve, the hum of human voices had been incessant, and where toil and labour had won support for so many.

Occasionally, the rude and reckless lumberman halts here, whilst his timber is passing the slide; the coarse jest and the coarser oath are alone heard at the falls of the Trent, save when the neighbouring farmer visits them, to procure a day's relaxation from his toils, and to view the grandeur of creation, and, we trust, to be thankful for the dispensation which has cast his lot in strange places. What must be the occasional thoughts of a man educated tenderly and luxuriously in England, when he reflects upon the changes and the chances which have brought him into contact with the domain of the bear, of the snake, and of the lumberer? Dear, dear England, thy green glades, thy peaceful villages, thy thousand comforts, the scenes of youth, the friends, the parents, who have gone to the land of promise—will these memories not intrude? No where in this wonderful world do they come upon the mind with more solemn impressiveness than in the wild woods of Canada.

CHAPTER XVIII.

Prospects of the Emigrant in Canada—Caution against ardent spirits and excessive smoking—Militia of Canada—Population—The mass of the Canadians soundly British—Rapidly increasing Prosperity of the North American Colonies, compared with the United States—Kingston—Its Commercial Importance—Conclusion.

It is time to take leave of the reader, and to say again some few parting words about the prospects which an emigrant will have before him in leaving the sacred homes of Britain, hallowed by the memories of ages, for a world and a country so new as Western Canada.

If the well-educated emigrant is determined to try his fortunes in Canada, let him choose either the eastern townships, in Lower Canada, or almost any portions of Canada West. I premise that he must have a little money at command; and, if possible, that either he, or some member of his family, have an annual income of at least fifty pounds, and that the young are healthy, and determined not to drink whiskey.

Drink not ardent spirits, for it is not necessary to strengthen or cheer you in labouring in the Bush. I am not an advocate for an educated man joining Temperance Societies, and look upon them as very great humbugs in many instances; but, with the uneducated, it is another affair altogether. If an educated man has not sufficient confidence in himself, and wishes to reduce himself to the degraded condition of an habitual drunkard, all the temperance pledges and sanctimonious tea-parties in the world will not eventually prevent him from wallowing in the mire. Father Matthew deserves canonizing for his bringing the Irish peasantry into the condition of a temperate people, but there religion is the vehicle; with Protestants such a vehicle should never be attempted, unless the clergy once more are the directors of conscience and of action, and could conscientiously absolve the taker of the pledge, should he fail. With the diversity of sects now existing in Protestantism, this would be obviously impracticable, and the attempt lead to a result one can hardly imagine without horror. No oath ought to be administered to a Protestant on such a subject; as, if a believer of that class of Christians should voluntarily take one and then break it, how much greater would his sin be than the sin of one who really and truly is convinced that a human being could pardon him, should he perjure himself!

The effects of drinking spirits in Canada are beyond anything I had imagined, until the report of the census of the Lower province for 1843, and that of Dr. Rees upon the lunatic asylum at Toronto, in the Upper, were published. The population of Lower Canada was 693,649, of which there were—

	Males.	Females.	Total.
Deaf and dumb	447	278	725
Blind	273	250	523
Idiots	478	472	950
Lunatics	156	152	308
Total	1354	1152	2506

The proportion of deaf and dumb to the whole population is as 1 to about 957: a greater proport

ion than prevails throughout all Europe (1 to 1537), United States (1 in 2000), or the whole world throughout (1 in 1556.)

The census of Upper Canada, taken a year before, gives the total population as 506,505. Of these there were—

	Males.	Females.	Total.
Deaf and dumb	222	132	354
Blind	114	89	203
Idiots	221	178	393
Lunatics	241	478	719
Total	798	877	1669

Thus, of a total population of 1,200,154, in 1833, there were 1027 persons confined in the provincial lunatic asylums, and perhaps a great many more out of them, as they have only just come into operation, and are still very inefficient. The idiots, it will appear, amounted to 1349.

In the whole North American continent, Canada is only exceeded by the States of New Hampshire and Connecticut, in the lists of insanity; and, to show that intemperance as well as climate has something to do with this melancholy result, I shall only state, without entering into details, that a well-informed resident has calculated that, when the province contained the above number of inhabitants, the consumption of alcoholic liquors, chiefly whiskey, was, excluding children under fifteen years of age, five gallons a year for every inhabitant; whilst, in 1843, in England and Wales, where the most accurate returns of the Excise prove the fact, it is only 0.69 of a gallon; in Scotland, 2.16; in Ireland, 0.64; and the total consumed by each individual, not excluding those under fifteen, is only 0.82 per annum for the three kingdoms. If the children under fifteen in Canada are to be included, still the consumption of spirit is awful, being 2¾ gallons for each; but it must be much higher, since the Excise is not regulated as at home.

That such excessive drinking prevails in Canada may be attributed partly to the cheapness of a vile mixture, called Canadian whiskey, and partly to climate, with a thermometer ranging to 120°, and with such rapid alternations. In Canada, also, man really conquers the earth by the sweat of his brow; for there is no harder labour than the preparation of timber, and the subduing of a primeval forest in a country of lakes and swamps.

I have an instance of the effect of excessive drinking daily before my door, in the person of a man of respectable family and of excellent talents, who, after habitually indulging himself with at last the moderate quantum of sixty glasses of spirits and water a day, now roams the streets a confirmed idiot, but, strange to say, never touches the cause of his malady. Are, therefore, not idiocy, madness, and perhaps two-thirds of the dreadful calamities to which human nature is subject here, owing to whiskey? I have seen an Irish labourer on the works take off at a draught a tumbler of raw whiskey, made from Indian corn or oats, to refresh himself; this would kill most men unaccustomed to it; but a corroded stomach it only stimulates.

Canada is a fine place for drunkards; it is their paradise—"Get drunk for a penny; clean straw for nothing" there. Think, my dear reader, of whiskey at tenpence a gallon—cheaper than water from the New River in London. Father Matthew, your principles are much wanted on this side of Great Britain.

Then, smoking to excess is another source of immense evil in the Backwoods. A man accustomed only to a cigar gets at last accustomed to the lowest and vilest of tobacco. I used to laugh at some of my friends in Seymour, when I saw them with a broken tobacco-pipe stuck in the ribbon of their straw hats. These were men who had paraded in their day the shady side of Pall Mall. They found a pipe a solace, and cigars were not to be had for love or money. "Why do you not put your pipe at least out of sight?" said I.

"It is the Seymour Arms' crest," responded my good-natured gentlemen farmers, "and we wear it accordingly."

Smoking all day, from the hour of rising, is, I actually believe, more injurious to the nerves than hard drinking. It paralyzes exertion. I never saw an Irish labourer, with his hod and his pipe, mounting a ladder, but I was sure to discover that he was an idler. I never had a groom that smoked much who took proper care of my horses; and I never knew a gentleman seriously addicted to smoking, who cared much for any thing beyond self. A Father Matthew pledge against the excessive use of tobacco would be of much more benefit among the labouring Irish than King James his Counterblast proved among the English.

The emigrant of education will naturally inquire, if, in case of war, he will be under the necessity of leaving his farm for the defence of the country.

The militia laws are now undergoing revision, in order to create an efficient force.

The militia of Western Canada are well composed, and have become a most formidable body of 80,000 men, [6] and are not to be classed with rude and undisciplined masses. In 1837, they rushed to the defence of their soil; and, so eager were they to attain a knowledge of the duties of a soldier, that, in the course of four months, many divisions were able to go through field-days with the regulars; and the embodied regiments, being clothed in scarlet, were always supposed by American visitors to be of the line.

There is a military spirit in this people, which only requires development and a good system of officer and sub-officer to make it shine. Any attempt to create partizan officers must be repressed, and merit and stake in the country alone attended to.

The population of the British provinces cannot now be less than nearly two millions; and it only requires judgment to bring forward the Canad'an French to insure their acting against an enemy daring to invade the country, as they so nobly did in 1812. I subjoin the latest correct census, 1844, of the Franco-Canadian race, as it will now be interesting in a high degree to the reader in Europe.

It is taken from a French Canadian journal of talent and resources, and agrees with the published authorities on this subject.

Population of Lower Canada in 1831 and 1844.—The following table of the comparative population of Lower Canada at the periods above-mentioned first appeared in the Canadien.

	1831.	1844.
Saguenay	8,385	13,445
Montmorency (1)	8,089	8,434
Quebec	36,173	45,676
Portneuf	13,656	15,922
Champlain	6,991	10,404
St. Maurice	16,909	20,594
Berthier	20,225	26,700
Leinster (2)	22,122	25,300
Terrebonne	16,623	20,646
Deux Montagnes	20,905	26,835
Outaouais	4,786	11,340
Montreal	43,773	64,306
Vaudreuil	13,111	16,616
Beauharnois	16,859	28,580
Huntingdon (3)	29,916	36,204
Rouville	18,115	20,098
Chambly	15,483	17,171
Vercheres	12,819	12,968
Richelieu	16,146	20,983
St. Hyacinthe	13,366	21,734
Shefford	5,087	9,996
Missisqoui	8,801	10,875
Stanstead	10,306	11,846
Sherbrooke	7,104	13,302
Drummond	3,566	9,374
Vamaska	9,495	11,645
Nicolet	12,509	16,280
Lothiniere	9,191	13,697
Megantic	2,283	6,730

Dorchester (4)		23,816	34,826
Bellechasse		13,529	14,540
L'Islet		13,518	16,990
Kamouraska		14,557	17,465
Rimouski		10,061	17,577
Gaspé		5,003	7,458
Bonaventure		8,109	8,230
		————	————
Total		511,919	678,590
In 1844			678,590
In 1831			511,919
			————
Augmentation in 13 years			166,671

The increase during the interval between the years cited is about 32½ per cent. It would no doubt have been more considerable but for the cholera, which in 1832 and 1834 decimated the population. The troubles of 1837-8 likewise contributed to check any increase; as, at those periods, numbers emigrated from this province to the United States, and the usual immigration from Europe hither was also materially interfered with.

Assuming 1,500,000 as the present actual population of the Canadas, we shall examine the strength of British North America from published returns in 1845, or the best authorities.

POPULATION, 1845.			CHIEF CITIES.	POP'N OF 1845
		{	Montreal	60,000
		{	Quebec	30,000
Canada	1,500,000	{	Kingston	12,000
		{	Toronto	20,000
		{	Fredericton	6,000
New Brunswick	200,000	{	St. John	6,000

Nova Scotia, including		{	Halifax	16,000
Cape Breton	250,000	{	Sydney	-----
Newfoundland	100,000		St. John's	20,000
Prince Edward's Island and the Magdalen Isles	45,000		Charlotte Town	-----
Total Population	2,095,000.			

A serviceable militia of 80,000 young men may, therefore, without distressing the population, be easily raised in British North America, with a reserve sufficient to keep an army of 40,000 able-bodied soldiers in Canada always in the field; and, if necessary, 100,000 could be assembled at any point, for any given purpose.

The Great Gustavus said that he would not desire a larger military force for defensive purposes than 40,000 men fit for actual service, to accomplish any military object, as such a force would always enable him to choose his positions. Two such armies of effective men could be easily maintained in the two Canadas, and concentrated rapidly and with certainty upon any given point, notwithstanding the extent of frontier; and the Canadians are much more essentially soldiers than the people of the United States, without any reference to valour or contempt of danger: whilst they would be fighting for everything dear to them, and the aggressors for mere extension of territory, and to accomplish the fixed object of destroying all monarchical institutions.

I have already said that there is no sympathy of the Irish settlers in Canada with the native Americans, and the best proof of this is the public demonstrations upon St. Patrick's day at Montreal, Kingston, and Toronto, where the two parties, Protestant and Catholic, exhibited no party emblems, no flags but loyal ones, and where the ancient enmity between the rival houses of Capulet and Montague, the Green and the Orange, appeared to have vanished before the approaching arrogant demands of a newly-erected Imperium.

Independence may exist to a great extent in Canada. Gourlay figured it, twenty years ago, by placing the word in capitals on the arch formed by the prismatic hues of the cloud-spray of Niagara. He could get no better ground than a fog-bank to hoist his flag upon, and the vision and the visionary have alike been swallowed up in oblivion.

Canada does not hate democracy so very totally and unequivocally as my excellent friend, Sir Francis Head, so tersely observed, but Canada repudiates annexation.

That a great portion of the population of this rapidly advancing colony feel a vast pride in imagining themselves about to become ranked among the nations of the world, I entertain not the shadow of a doubt; but that the physical and moral strength of Canada desire immediate separation from England, or annexation to the republic presided over by President Polk, is about as absurd a chimera as that of Gourlay and the spray of Niagara. The rainbow there, splendid as it is, owes its colours to the sun.

The mass in Canada is soundly British; and, having weighed the relative advantages and disadvantages of British principles and laws with those of the United States, the beam of the latter has mounted into the thin air of Mr. Gourlay's vision. The greatest absurdity at present discoverable is in the ideas of unfortunate individuals, who imagine themselves placed near the pivot desired by the philosopher, and that they possess the lever which is to move the solid globe to any position into which it may suit them to upheave it.

A poor man by origin, and with some talent, suddenly becomes the Sir Oracle of his village; and, because the Governor-General does not advance his protégé or connexions, or because he does not imagine that the welfare of the province hinges upon his support, turns sulky, and obtaining, by very easy means, a seat in the Assembly, becomes all at once an ultra on the opposite side of the question.

In all new countries ambition gets the better of discretion, but fortunately soon finds its natural level: the violent ultra-tory, and the violent ultra-demagogue sink alike, after a few years of excitement, into the moth-eaten receptacle of newspaper renown, alike unheeded, and alike forgotten, by a newer and more enlightened generation, who find that, to the cost of the real interest of the people, the mouthing orator, the agitator, the exciter, is not the patriot.

Canada, although emphatically a new country, is rapidly becoming a most important one, and increasing with a vigour not contemplated in England. It is proved, by ample statistical details, that the United States is behind-hand, ceteris paribus, in the race.

The thirteen colonies declared their independence in 1783, now only sixty-three years, and amply within the memory of men. The following data for 1784 may be compared to 1836:—

1784.

	Imports.	Exports.	Population.	Shipping Tons.
Nova Scotia }				
Cape Breton }	£75,000	£3,500	32,000	12,000
St. John's }				
Prince Edward's Island}				
Canada	500,000	150,000	113,000	95,000
Newfoundland	80,000	70,000	20,000	20,000
Total	£655,000	£223,500	165,000	127,000

1836.

Or just before the disturbances in Canada, and before the Union.

	Imports.	Exports.	Population.	Shipping Tons.
Nova Scotia	£1,245,000	£935,000	150,000	374,000
Canada	2,580,000	1,321,750	1,200,000	348,000
Newfoundland	632,576	850,344	70,000	98,000
Cape Breton	80,000	90,000	35,000	70,000
Prince Edward's Island	46,000	90,000	32,000	23,800
New Brunswick	250,000	700,000	164,000	347,000
Total	£4,833,576	£3,987,094	1,651,000	1,260,800

THE UNITED STATES.

	Imports.	Exports.	Population.	Shipping Tons.
1784	£4,250,000	£1,000,000	3,000,000	500,000
1836	162,000,000	121,000,000	15,000,000	2,000,000

Thus the increase in shipping alone to the North American colonies, compared with the United States, was as ten to four, and the increase of population as ten to three.

In imports, the United States, compared with the colonies in that period, increased as 40 to 9, exports 120 to 19; but then the Americans had the whole world for customers, and the colonies Great Britain only, until very lately, and then, even in the West India trade, they could scarcely compete with their rivals; whereas the Americans started with four times the shipping, nearly double the population, six times the import, and four times the export trade, and the people of the republic had already occupied at least ten great commercial ports, whilst Quebec, Halifax, and St. John, were yet in infancy as mercantile entrepôts.

Passing over all but Western Canada, we shall examine the state of that province after the rebellion of 1839, when Lord Durham informed us that

The population was	513,000,	
Value of fixed }		{An increase of two
and assessed }	£5,043,253	{millions and a
property }		{quarter in ten years.
Cultivated acres	1,738,500	
Grist-mills	678	
Saw-mills	933	
Cattle	400,000	

and yet Upper Canada was only a howling wilderness in 1784.

It is now supposed, upon competent authority, that the British possessions north of New York contain not fewer than two millions and a quarter of inhabitants, a fixed and floating capital of seventy-five million pounds, a public revenue of a million and a quarter, with a tonnage of not less than two millions and a quarter, manned, including the lake craft, steamboats, and fishing-vessels, by one hundred and fifty thousand sailors; and this Western Britain consumes annually seven millions of pounds sterling of British goods.

The Inspector-General of Revenue for Canada alone gives us the following data:—

1845.	
Revenue of Canada	£524,637
Expenditure	500,839

Now let us see what the Standing Army and Militia of the United States are in 1845:

Standing Army—7,590 officers and men, including all ranks.

Militia—627 Generals, 2,670 Staff-officers, 13,813 Field-officers, 44,938 Company-officers, and 1,385,645 men.

Naval Force—11 ships of the line, 14 first-class frigates, 17 sloops-of-war, 8 brigs, 9 schooners, 6 steamers: with 67 captains, 94 commanders, 324 lieutenants, 133 passed midshipmen, 416 midshipmen, and 31 masters.

The crews being formed of European sailors chiefly, no estimate is given of sufficient authenticity to depend upon as to the native citizens employed afloat in the services of the State.

The Militia appears a fearful Xerxian force, but it is really of no consequence whatever except as a protective one for the purposes of invasion, being quite met by the militia of the British provinces, as no larger army than 20,000 men can be effectually moved or subsisted on such an extensive frontier as Canada, and that only by an immense sacrifice of money.

Having thus given a glimpse at the state of affairs, I must leave my readers for the present, after a little talk about the city of Kingston.

Kingston, instead of suffering, as predicted, by the removal of the seat of government, having been thrown on her own resources, is rising fast.

Her naval and commercial harbours are being strongly fortified. The public buildings are important and handsome.

The Town Hall is probably the finest edifice of the kind on the continent of America, and cost £30,000, containing two splendid rooms of vast size, Post-office, Custom-house, Commercial Newsroom, shops, and a complete Market Place, with Mayor's Court and Policeoffice, and a lofty cupola, commanding a view of immense extent.

There are three English churches, built of stone, a Scots church of the same material, several dissenting places of worship, and a magnificent cathedral, almost equal in size to that at Montreal, for Roman Catholics, with a smaller church attached, a seminary for educating the priests, a nunnery, and an Hotel Dieu, conducted by Sisters of Charity; also an immense building for a public hospital, extensive barracks for troops, and several private houses of inferior importance, with four banks.

There are ten daily first-class steamers running to and from Kingston, and about thirty smaller steamers and propellers, with a fleet of two hundred schooners and sailing barges. The navigation is open from the 1st of April until late in November.

To show the trade of this rising city, now containing near twelve thousand inhabitants, I append a table of its Exports and Imports, for 1845.

IMPORTS AND DUTIES, AT KINGSTON, FOR 1845.

Articles Imported.	Number or quantity.	Value at the place of import.			Amount of all Duties.			Remarks.
		£	s.	d.	£	s.	d.	
Animals—								
Cows and Heifers	No. 12	54	10	0	14	12	0	
Horses, Mares} Geldings } Colts, Fillies }	" 13	231	5	0	23	14	6	
Foals	" 21	222	10	0	-	-	-	Of traveller
Lambs	" 70	16	0	0	3	5	2	
Oxen, Bulls, Steers	" 202	1514	0	0	406	19	6	
Pigs(sucking)	" 1	0	5	0	0	0	7	
Swine and Hogs	" 1212	3474	10	2	368	13	0	
Sheep	" 337	90	8	9	41	0	0	
Anchovies & Sardines	in oil	3	0	6	0	7	10	
Ashes, barrels	67	279	7	9	13	9	8	
Bark		99	16	0	4	17	8	
Berries, Nuts, Vegetables	for dying	156	16	5	12	13	9	
Biscuits and Crackers		111	11	10	10	4	6	
Books		1329	6	1	150	12	9	Private library

Item	Unit	Quantity			Value						Notes
Do.					20	0	0	-	-	-	from Europe
Candles—Sperm	lb.	3,770			310	6	10	84	13	3	Bonded for
Wax	"	3,457			163	11	10	28	19	3	lower ports
Other kinds	"	13,800			856	11	3	-	-	-	
Carriages, Vehicles	No.	28			220	0	0	18	13	5	Of travellers
Do.	No.	20			256	5	0	-	-	-	
Clocks and Watches					1046	7	1	157	7	2	
Coals	tons.	373	0	76	515	12	11	23	17	1	
Cocoa	cwt.		1	20	1	18	0	0	2	11	
Coffee—Green	cwt.	288	8	1	625	17	10	247	2	4	Removed
Do.	cwt.	27	1	9	66	0	0	-	-	-	under bond
Roasted	"	13	1	1	30	18	10	19	1	11	to Hamilton
Ground	"	8	0	20	15	19	9	21	1	8	
Coin and Bullion		22,500			0	0		-	-	-	
Cordage	cwt.	193	0	13	535	6	8	61	16	1	
Corks	gross	1086			80	11	8	9	6	0	
Cotton Manufactures					1,728	16	1	200	1	0	
Cotton Wool					236	0	0	11	16	0	
Drugs					327	13	6	17	0	10	
Extracts, Essences and Perfumery					92	1	3	12	0	0	
Fanning and Bark Mills		10			33	16	6	4	18	11	
Fins and Skins, the produce of creatures living in the sea					33	13	9	7	11	0	
Fish—Fresh, not described					260	11	3	6	11	7	

Article	Unit	Quantity			Value			Duty			Notes
Oysters, Lobsters and Turtles					1,100	14	9	7	11	0	
Salted or dried	cwt.	154	0	19	127	4	0	20	1	4	
Pickled	barls.	30			54	11	4	7	16	11	
Flour, Wheat	bar- {	8,396½			9,296	18	3	1,276	16	9	
	r e l s of {	204			224	8	0	7	16	11	Supplied H.M.
	1 9 6 lb. {	44,151			54,919	7	6	-	-	-	Commissariat
Fruit—Almonds	barls.	15,115			137	17	6	31	8	7	
Apples	bushels	13,966½			1,300	3	7	424	16	7	
Do. dried	"	163			36	14	7	11	7	4	
Currants	cwt.	47	3	24	105	10	9	18	2	1	
Figs	"	20	2	20	53	7	2	8	8	1	
Nuts	lb. {	9,421			140	17	1	29	10	4	
	{	610			6	2	0	-	-	-	Bonded for removal to
Pears	bushels	421¾			59	12	8	25	12	6	
Prunes	lb.	543			20	12	6	3	11	6	Hamilton.
Raisins in boxes	"	34,411			788	9	8	205	19	6	
Do., otherwise than in boxes	lb.	7,990			127	6	6	25	7	10	
Fur Skins, or Peltries undressed					22	16	6	1	2	5	
Glass Manufactures					860	3	11	168	0	1	
Grain, &c.—Barley	qrs.	373¾			369	4	9	68	4	2	
Maize, or Ind. Corn quarters	4 8 0 lb.	2,617½			2,717	13	9	477	15	9	
Oats	quarters	87½			43	13	9	10	12	11½	
Rye	quarters	69¾			51	19	7	12	13	6½	
Beans	quarters	2			4	8	0	0	7	3	

Meal of the above grs. and of Wheat not bolted, per 196 lb.		10½			4	10	0	15	6
Wheat	quarters	2,597¼			4,647	17	4	474	0	0
Bran & Shorts	cwt.	4	0	0	3	7	3	0	1	3
Gums and Resins					181	1	5	9	3	3
Hardware					3,883	2	10	466	11	4
Hay	tons	34½			56	1	3	12	11	10
Hemp, Flax & Tow	cwt. {	4,879	1	18	2,188	12	7	21	17	9
	" {	1,540	2	0	838	10	0	-	-	-
Hides, Raw	No.	755			338	3	9	3	7	8
Hops	lb.	936			26	0	6	15	5	6
India Rubber Boots & Shoes	pairs	936 1,197			218	1	7	45	6	6
Leather— Goat Skins, tanned or in any way dressed	doz.	4			6	12	0	1	9	7
Lamb and Sheep Skins	doz.	172			117	9	10	30	19	8
Calf Skins	lb.	857¼			90	18	5	29	13	10
Kid Skins	lb.	1,024			92	18	9	10	6	11
Harness Leather	"	12,641½			347	1	0	141	18	3
Upper Leather	"	4,109¾			271	7	11	51	9	3
Sole Leather	"	74,931			2,561	5	3	672	4	6
Leather not described					334	16	5	28	17	6
Leather Manufactures:									

Bonded for lower ports

Description	Unit	Quantity	£	s	d	£	s	d
Boots, Shoes, Calashes								
Women's Boots, Shoes, & Calashes of Leather	doz. prs.	52½	116	1	3	29	12	9
Girls' Boots, Shoes & Calashes under 7 in. in length of Leather	doz. prs.	38	38	12	3	8	14	6
Girls' Boots & Shoes of Silk, Satin, Jean or other stuff. Kid, Morocco	doz. prs.	14	20	14	7	3	12	2
Men's Boots of Leather	pairs	2,047	494	15	7	109	14	6
Men's Shoes, do.	"	161	29	7	1	11	18	2
Boy's Boots under 8 inches long	pairs	38	7	0	0	3	6	3
Boy's Shoes, do.	"	28	6	8	7	1	13	1
Leather Manufactures not described			330	19	2	38	4	6
Linen Manufactures			82	6	0	9	9	11
Liquids— Cider and Perry	gallons	5,679	61	15	5	32	1	7
Vinegar	"	2,670	87	2	2	44	4	0
Maccaroni and Vermicelli	lb.	493	13	18	2	3	1	1
Machinery			1,478	14	7	225	11	0

Article	Quantity				£	s.	d.	£	s.	d.
Mahogany and Hardwood, unmanufactured for Furniture					144	19	5	1	9	2
Manures of all kinds					29	12	6	0	1	0
Medicines					642	1	6	55	6	4
Molasses and Treacle	cwt.	193	2	8	141	10	6	47	1	7
Oakum	"		0	22	1	4	9	0	1	9
Oils—Olive, in casks	gallons	700			142	9	0	19	17	11
Do. in jars and bottles	gallons	56½			24	2	1	4	8	1
Lard	"	690			130	9	4	19	4	2
Linseed, raw or boiled	"	2,367			329	2	6	37	3	4
Oils,Vegetable,Volatile,Chemical,and Essential	gallons	131			58	18	3	6	9	9
Palm	"	150			23	6	6	1	2	11
The produce of Fish and creatures living in the sea	gals.	8,196½			1,941	12	7	309	16	2
Unenumerated	"	2,957¼			460	7	2	52	16	6
Paper Manufactures, other than Books & Playing Cards Pickles and Sauces					12	8	10	1	12	4
Playing Cards	packs				8	7	7	1	7	0
Potatoes	bushels	172½			12	5	3	2	12	6
Poultry and Game, live					9	1	0	0	18	1
Ditto, dead					63	2	4	8	9	9

Provisions—Butter	cwt.	3	3	9	13	1	3	2	16	11
Cheese	cwt.	248	2	22	400	9	3	113	9	3
Eggs	dozen	236			5	18	0	0	16	6
Lard	cwt.	40	1	18	90	18	0	3	19	5
Meats—Bacon and Hams	"	47	2	17	78	18	13	28	2	8½
Ditto, other Meats salted, &c.	cwt.	14,035	2	3	25,137	11	6	4,274	9	7
Ditto	"	4,237	2	20	5,656	0	0	-	-	-
Ditto, Fresh	"	261	3	15	264	14	9	63	14	0
Rice	"	282	2	0	350	17	4	17	9	2
Salt barls. of 280 lb.		975			255	14	2	148	5	8
Sausages & Puddings		975			0	3	4	0	0	6
Seeds					123	15	3	10	10	1
Silk Manufactures					136	9	10	26	13	4
Soap	cwt.	36	2	25	131	5	9	14	15	7
Spices—Cassia	lb.	305½			17	9	0	3	15	9
Cinnamon	"	160			9	18	6	2	0	3
Cloves	"	46			3	11	10	0	11	9
Nutmegs	"	2			0	13	9	0	1	4
Pepper of all kinds	"	1,254			34	1	4	4	10	9
Spirits and Cordials except Rum.— Not exceeding Proof,	gallons	32			4	10	0	4	7	7
Over proof,	"	16			2	5	0	2	3	9
Sweetened or mixed	"	7			10	17	6	1	5	6
Sugar—	cwt.	55	2	6½	164	3	9	95	18	3
Unrefined & Bastard	"	2,650	0	16	3,698	0	8	2,199	4	6

Bonded lower ports

Article	Unit	Quantity			£	s	d	£	s	d	
Syrups	"	137			45	4	6	7	9	2	Do.
Stearine	lb.	3,681			184	1	0	-	-	-	Do.
Tallow	cwt.	3,096	1	5½	5,385	17	6	53	1	3	
Tea	lb.	196,268			18,110	9	8	1,999	16	8	
Tobacco— Unmanufactured	"	1,923			222	18	9	-	-	-	
Do.	"	357			13	2	2	2	7	2	
Manufactured	"	202,508½			4,291	13	0	1,205	8	11	
Segars	"	1,627			550	12	10	236	12	11	
Snuff	"	1,981			87	19	7	46	6	8	
Trees, Shrubs, Plants, & Roots					222	0	11	8	17	6	
Settlers' Goods	lots	3			26	5	0	-	-	-	
Vegetables, except potatoes, fresh					334	6	6	36	13	4	
Wines	doz. gallons	1,162½			419	4	9	112	16	11	
Wines	doz. gallons	1,162½			419	4	9	112	16	11	
Wood, except Saw Logs & Mahogany. Pine, White	cubic ft.	11,750			147	12	7	17	17	3	
Oak	"	1,497			25	0	0	5	0	5	
Staves,Puncheon, or W. I. Standard std. M.	cubic ft.	57			609	13	5	86	7	0	
White Oak	"	435			1,442	3	2	263	0	1	
Handspikes	doz.	5			1	17	6	0	1	6	
Oars	pairs	17			3	14	3	0	5	5	
Planks,Boards,sawed Lumber	foot	40,473			89	4	0	17	13	0	
Woolen Manufactures					1,097	12	10	124	7	7	
Wood, Firewood	cords	397½			56	12	3	3	6	0	
All other articles not											

included under any of the foregoing heads	6,502	12	3	555	7	1
	— — — —	—	—	— — —	—	—
Totals, Currency	211,705	0	11	19,917	17	0

[Amount of duty on Imports bonded for lower ports--£8036 0 8]

Below, we give a return of the amount and value of goods imported at this Port through the United States, for the benefit of drawback. The importations under this law have not been large, but the return shows that a material saving has been effected under this operation. For the return we are indebted to the politeness of the late collector, Mr. Kirkpatrick.

AGGREGATE OF IMPORTS INTO KINGSTON FOR BENEFIT OF DRAWBACK.

Articles.	Quantity in Weight, &c.		Value.			Duties.			Drawback.	
			£	s.	d.	£	s.	d.	Dollars.	
Cigars	1,281	lbs.	404	8	4	184	3	3	502	43
Almonds	5,964	"	101	19	4	41	1	3	159	75
Currants	5,259	"	105	10	9	18	12	1	120	81
Raisins	39,216	"	844	11	4	217	18	1	1,059	86
Molasses	147	cwt. 3 qr. 4 lb.	109	3	0	35	19	18	72	66
Olive Oil	700	gallons	142	9	0	19	17	10	136	50
Linseed Oil	2,100	"	28	19	6	32	12	2	511	88
Raw Sugar	2,168	cwt. 2 qr. 8 lb.	3,169	6	3	1,889	13	10	5,899	74
Refined Sugar	6,020	lbs.	157	5	6	92	9	9	205	44
Wine	400	gallons	240	7	0	54	17	11	245	81
									8,914	91
			5,558	0	0	2,587	5	10	2,228	146

We have also been favoured with a return of the shipping, which, during the season of 1845, has entered this port. The reports to the Custom House embrace 388,788. This return includes the steamers employed on the Bay and Lake, when carrying merchandize; but, as the law requiring vessels to report only came into force several weeks after the opening of the navigation, and as it has not in all instances been obeyed, the return is not quite as full as it might have been under other circumstances. As much as 15,000 or 20,000 tons have in this way entered without reporting. The amount of tonnage for 1845, stated above, is likewise exclusive of all that engaged n trade on the canal and river, and which is very nearly equal in amount.

The Provincial Revenue returns for 1845 are said to exceed those of 1844 by £55,000.

Kingston is, in fact, the key of the Great Lakes, the St. Lawrence and the Rideau Canal being their outlets for commerce; but, unless railroads are established between the Atlantic at Halifax and these Lakes, the prosperity of this and many other inland towns will be materially affected, as by the enlargement of the Rideau branches at Grenville, &c. and the La Chine Canal to the required ship navigation size, Kingston must no longer hope for the unshipment of bulky goods and the forwarding trade on which she so mainly depends; a glance at the forwarding business done by the Erie Canal to New York on the American side, and that by the Welland, St. Lawrence, and Rideau on the Canadian, being quite sufficient to prove that all the energies of the Canadians are required to compete with their rivals. And for this purpose I cite an extract from a circular put forth by the Free Trade Association of Montreal, which contains a good deal of sound reasoning on this subject, amidst, of course, much party feeling on the Free Trade principle.

"We now proceed, in the development of our plan, to show the incalculable advantages that will result to Canadian commerce and the carrying trade, by removing all duties and restrictions from American produce.

"First, we shall show the amount of produce collected annually on the shores of our great island waters, and brought to this city for distribution to the various markets of consumption; next, the vast quantity that passes through the Erie Canal, seeking a market at New York and other American ports; and, lastly, we shall show that it is in the power of Canada to divert a large share of this latter trade through her own waters, if her people and legislature will promptly give effect to the liberal and enlarged policy which it is the object of this Association to advocate and urge.

"NO. 1.—SHOWING THE QUANTITY OF PRODUCE BROUGHT BY THE ST. LAWRENCE TO THE CITY OF MONTREAL, IN THE YEAR 1845:—

"Pork, 6,109 barrels; beef, 723 barrels; lard, 460 kegs; flour, 590,305 barrels; wheat, 450,209 bushels; other grain, 40,781 bushels; ashes, 33,000 barrels; butter, 8,112 kegs.

"NO. 2.—SHOWING THE QUANTITY OF PRODUCE CARRIED THROUGH THE ERIE CANAL IN THE YEAR 1844:—

"Pork, 63,646 barrels; beef, 7,699 barrels; lard, 3,064,800 lbs.; flour, 2,517,250 barrels; wheat, 1,620,033 bushels; corn, 35,803 bushels; flax-seed, 8,303,960 lbs.; ashes, 80,646 barrels.

"From the foregoing statements it will be seen that the quantity carried through the latter channel is enormous as compared with the former. It becomes then a question of vital importance whether a portion of this trade can be attracted through the St. Lawrence. We believe that it can, because the cheapest conveyance to the seaboard and to the manufacturing districts of New England must win the prize; and who will deny that the securing of this prize is not worth both our best and united exertions?

"The cheapening of the means of transit is the great object to be obtained; and our best practical authorities are firmly of opinion that the St. Lawrence will be made the cheapest route, as soon as our chain of inland improvements is rendered complete. They affirm that the cost of transporting a barrel of flour from Detroit to Montreal will not exceed 1s. 6d. to 1s. 9d. The difficulty will then be to secure a port of constant access to the sea, and that difficulty will be overcome by the early completion of the projected Portland railway: a road that will place us within a day's journey of that city, the harbour of which may be made the safest and cheapest on the continent of America. By that route we shall avoid the occasional dangers and inconveniencies of the St. Lawrence, from Montreal outwards, practically secure a long season for trade in the fall of the year, and safely reckon on freights to Liverpool as low as those from New York. But what is equally important to the transit trade to England is this: that by rendering our charges cheaper than those through the Erie Canal to Boston, we shall secure the transit trade to that great city, and all other eastern markets, as well as the supplying of our sister colonies, commonly known as the Lower Ports. This picture may appear too flattering to those who have not investigated the subject; but to such we say, examination will convince them that, with the St. Lawrence as a highway, and Portland as an outlet to the sea, we shall be enabled, successfully, to struggle for the mighty trade of the West, and bid defiance to competition on the more artificial route of the Erie Canal. But there is no time for slumbering; inactivity, at this crisis, would be fatal to our hopes; even the very produce of Western Canada may be carried, in spite of us, through American channels, unless we immediately carry out the completion of our own.

"We may here also remind the Canadian farmer, at whatever place he may be situated, that every saving effected in the means of bringing his produce to market adds in the same degree to the value of his wheat and every other marketable product of the soil he cultivates.—And here it may not be out of place to add that, repudiating all sectional proceedings, we seek no advantage for classes, no peculiar advantage for Montreal over other parts of the province; we advocate, on the contrary, the general interests of producers and consumers—the general welfare of the community."

People of enlarged views in Canada do not, however, fancy, with the anti-free-traders, that Sir Robert Peel's measures will prove so very destructive to colonial interests; on the contrary, they clearly see that new energies will be called into operation, and that Canada will be opened by railroads, and no longer monopolized by extensive landholders of waste and unprofitable forests.

Having now arrived at the termination of this volume, I have only to add that, if a war is forced upon Great Britain by the United States, the British dominion here will be sustained without flinching; and that the old English aspiration of the militia will be

FOR THE HONOUR AND GLORY OF BRITAIN,

GOD SAVE THE QUEEN!

[1] I think, however, I have read that the philosophic printer gave him a very bad character.

[2] A large public meeting of Roman Catholics upon the subject of the University question took place lately at Toronto, where a temperate spirit prevailed.

[3] Brown Bess, a musket—vide Infantry Dictionary.

[4] Team is called in Canada and in the States a span of horses, and means two.

[5] In crossing the Atlantic in an American packet with a highly-gifted American, he told me one day that he was really glad to observe that such excellent dockyards were making at Bermuda, as in a few years they would no doubt belong to the Union. This was not said boastingly, but seriously.

[6] Eastern and Western Canada comprise an able-bodied militia of 160,000.